God bless!

Love,
Tammy Christy

L.I.F.E. Apps

Devotions for Living in Faith Every Day

Tammy Dozier Trusty

L.I.F.E. Apps
Devotions for Living in Faith Every Day
By: Tammy Dozier Trusty
Edited by: Terah Trusty
Cover Art by: Tina Swinford

Published by: From the Heart Books LLC
United States

ISBN 9781733335102
Library of Congress Control Number 2019914241

Amplified Bible, The Lockman Foundation, 1999-2015.

The Living Bible, Tyndale House Publishers, Inc, 1971.

New International Version, Biblica, 2011-2016.

NIV Once-A-Day Bible for Women, Zondervan, 2012.

The Message, NavPress Publishing Group, 2002.

Thank you to my daughter, Terah, for all her hard work editing, organizing, and working on this book with me. I couldn't have done it without you.

Thank you, Tina, for the beautiful cover art!

Thank you, Sandra Pavloff Conner, for all your help!

I dedicate all my writing and
my life to my Lord and Savior, Jesus.

This book is dedicated to my loving husband.
Thank you for your love and support through all the years.
I love you!

"So, go now and write all this down.
Put it in a book so that the record will be there
to instruct the coming generations"
(*The Message,* Isaiah 30.8).

"For everything that was written in the
past was written to teach us, so that
through the endurance taught in the
Scriptures and the encouragement they
provide we might have hope"
(*New International Version*, Romans 15.4).

Table of Contents

Introduction

Writing has always been a passion of mine. Growing up, I wrote many poems, especially as a teenager. I even had one published in my church quarterly. Later, I bought a book of poems that had one of mine printed in it. Listening to music helped me to write. I remember listening to music like Carole King, James Taylor, or The Carpenters while writing.

Early in 2014, I was asked to help write devotions for my church. The devotions would go along with the sermons for the year. A short devotion would be easy for me to do since I have done it many times, but the difference was that they wanted us to include a short personal story to go along with the lesson. I almost refused because I didn't think I could write true stories about myself. I found that I liked doing it, especially writing about my life. I decided that would be a great way to share my life with my family. I decided to write more devotions and make a book for my family. May you enjoy, be strengthen, equipped, and encouraged to live by faith every day as you read this collection of devotions.

Blessings,

Tammy Dozier Trusty

Chapter 1: Seeking God

Spending Time with God

Read Ephesians 6: 1-4; Colossians 3:18-21, "Be still and know that I am God" (*New International Version*, Psalm 46.10).

As parents, we are often too busy living life, working, raising our children, and just getting through the day to stop and reflect. Times of quiet are few and far between. I spoke to a young mother the other day encouraging her to get in the Word and pray. She said that she just doesn't have the time. She said the children even follow her to the bathroom.

I am not an early bird, but I find that it's easier to get up a little earlier and start my day with the Word and in prayer. It's a great way to begin the day, and then everything seems to fall into place. If difficult things come up, I can get through them easier because I have spent time with God. Carving out a little time with God is vital. Spending time with God each day gives us strength, wisdom, and grace for the day.

Prayer:

Heavenly Father, I want to spend time with You. Help me to find time to spend with You. Give me creative ways to have more time. I know that I need time to pray and study the scriptures. I love you, Lord. In Jesus' name, I pray. Amen.

Worship

Read Acts 2.

"And when the day of Pentecost was fully come, they were all with one accord in one place" (*New International Version*, Acts 2.1).

Last year, we took our grown children and grandchildren to see the St. Louis Cardinals play baseball. About 100 people from our community all went, too. Everywhere you looked there was a sea of red Cardinal shirts and hats. We cheered when there was a hit or an out. We sang "Take me out to the Ballgame." It was fun being in a stadium filled with mostly Cardinal fans all focused on one thing.

In Acts 2, the disciples were all praying, waiting, and focusing on God together. Then the power of God showed up. We should focus on God and see what happens. Are you focusing your time and energy on God? Most people think that you can live your life like you want and give God the leftovers. Instead, we should focus on God and do His will.

Prayer:

Lord God, thank You that I can know You as my Lord and God. Help me to put You first in my life. Help me to focus on You and do Your will, so I am pleasing to You. May my life, thoughts, and the meditations of my heart be pleasing and acceptable to You. I pray in Jesus' name. Amen.

Wise Men Still Seek Him

Read Luke 2: 9-20.

"And, lo, the star, which they saw in the east, went before them, till it came and stood over where the young child was. When they saw the star, they rejoiced with exceeding great joy. And when they were come into the house, they saw the young child with Mary his mother, and fell down, and worshipped him: and when they had opened their treasures, they presented unto him gifts; gold, and frankincense and myrrh" (*King James Version,* Matthew 2.9-11).

Each Christmas, my mom and dad put out a big plastic nativity set with Mary, Joseph, Baby Jesus, and a large star. This Christmas, they prepared to put it in front of the house again. My mom bought a pre-made wooden stable for it. She was ready to start putting out her decorations, so she sent my dad after the nativity set. The problem was that my dad couldn't find it. He looked through their huge garage and the shed. It's a hard item to lose because the parts are big. Each part is at least two foot each, and they were in a large box. For days, we heard that the baby Jesus was lost. They couldn't find him. Each conversation started out, "Did you look here? Did you look there? Where could it be?" For days my parents were seeking Jesus.

Today we say, "Wise men still seek him." Even though my parents were literally seeking the plastic figures, they were seeking Jesus. People still seek God in their own ways. The shepherds and the Magi followed the star to find Jesus. We should seek Him, too. Each day of our lives, we should seek to do His will, to surrender more and more to Him, to let Him influence and guide our decisions, and to seek and save the lost. Seeking Jesus when your life is in turmoil, will give you peace and comfort. Let us seek Him each and every day, not just around Christmas!

Prayer:

Dear Heavenly Father, thank you for being born, dying on the cross for my sins, and for giving Your Holy Spirit to us. Seeking and finding You is the best decision that I have ever made. May I seek You each and every day of my life. I surrender my life to You. In Jesus' name. Amen.

P.S. The nativity set was stored up in the garage rafters! What was lost now is found!

Keeping Christ in Christmas

Read Luke 2; Isaiah 9:6

"Behold, a virgin shall be with child, and shall bring forth a son, and they shall call his name Emmanuel, which being interpreted is, God with us. Then Joseph being raised from sleep did as the angel of the Lord had bidden him, and took unto him his wife: And knew her not till she had brought forth her firstborn son: and he called his name Jesus" (*New International Version*, Matthew 1.23).

There is a big debate about saying, "Merry Christmas." It really does leave Jesus out of the picture if you just say, "Happy Holidays." Another thing we say this time of year is "Jesus is the reason for the season." However, I think we often just say it and not really think about it. It's not a cliché. He really IS the very reason we have Christmas!

I know some of my holiday gatherings should be more Christ centered because presents usually take center stage. One of the things we used to do each year is have a birthday cake for Jesus. We would gather the kids around and sing, "Happy Birthday" to Jesus. At my family's celebration, I often read the Christmas story from Luke 2. One year, I let the younger children put the nativity in place as I read. One year, I got a nice plastic set for the younger kids and put it under the tree. They loved to play with it, especially Baby Jesus. Keeping Christ in Christmas is important if you are a Christ follower.

Keeping Christ in Christmas isn't just for the holidays; it is for each and every day. He should be the center of our lives. Our lives should be influenced by the Word of God and the life of Jesus. He spent His days helping others. We should too. Don't take Christ out of Christmas this year. Keep Him in your life each day! Daily acknowledgment of Christ will bring you hope, joy, and peace!

Prayer:

Dear Heavenly Father God, thank You for sending Your Son, Jesus, here on earth for the atonement of our sins. Thank you for His sacrifice. May it ever be on my mind. May I never take it for granted. Serving and loving Jesus is what I want to do each day of my life. Help me to be more aware of You in my life each day. Forgive me for taking You for granted. Forgive me for neglecting to spend time with You. Forgive me for being self-absorbed and self-centered. Change me, Lord. Help me to keep Christ in Christmas. In Jesus' name. Amen.

Encounter with Jesus

Read Matthew 1-2; Luke 2.

Now when the centurion, and they that were with him, watching Jesus, saw the earthquake, and those things that were done, they feared greatly, saying, "Truly this was the Son of God." (*King James Version*, Matthew 27:54)

The innkeeper encountered Jesus because Mary was pregnant with Him, but he sent them away to the barn. He didn't recognize the significance of Jesus. Hopefully, after Jesus' birth, the innkeeper had an encounter with the Most High God!

Angels visited the shepherds to tell of His birth. The angels proclaimed His birth, so the shepherds followed the star to the stable. They had a double encounter, first, with the angels. Imagine the sight of that! Then they encountered the Christ child in a manger. Imagine their awe to be told of His birth and to see Him in person. What a humbling encounter with Jesus!

The wise men were seeking the Christ child by following the star. Even though He was in a manger in a stable born from lowly Mary, they recognized Him as the Messiah. They encountered their Messiah!

Separately Simeon and Anna each encountered Jesus after His birth. They had been waiting a lifetime to see Him. They recognized Him as the King of Kings. The worshiped Him. They encountered the long-awaited Messiah!

When the Roman soldier encountered Jesus on the cross. He recognized Him as the Son of God after His sacrifice on the cross. He encountered the Son of God (*New International Version*, Matthew 27.54).

Each of them encountered Jesus. Each one of them recognized Him. Each one worshiped Him. Each one was changed by the encounter. When we encounter Jesus, recognize Him, and worship Him, it changes our lives. Meet Jesus, the

Most High God, the Christ Child, the Messiah, the King of Kings, and the Son of God. When you encounter Jesus, your life changes forever!

Prayer:

Father God, thank you that I had an encounter with Jesus long ago. Thank you that I can continue to encounter Him daily. May I continue to recognize, surrender, and worship Him as the Lord of my life. May my friends and family have an encounter with Jesus that changes their lives forever. Bring them revelation of what Jesus did on the cross, His sacrifice for us, and God's love. I ask in Jesus' precious name. Amen.

Chapter 2: Identity in Christ

Our Identity in Christ

Read Romans 8.

"...You have received a spirit of adoption as sons by which we cry out, 'Abba! Father!' The Spirit Himself testifies with our spirit that we are children of God, and if children, heirs also, heirs of God and fellow heirs with Christ" (*New International Version*, Romans 8.15-17).

Growing up, I always had long, thick, wavy, dark brown almost black hair. When I was small, my mom would curl my hair in long banana curls. Wherever I went people commented on my beautiful hair until I got it cut. My hair was me; I always thought it defined who I was. At the time, I didn't feel like I had any other redeeming qualities, so without a long mane of hair, I felt upset and lost. Now I know who I am in Christ, and it has nothing to do with my hair.

Now I know that my identity is in Jesus Christ, my Savior and Lord. Unknowingly for many years, I believed lies about myself; I had low self-esteem. I never realized that Jesus redeemed me from the curse of the law, so I am redeemed. He brought me into the family of God, so I am God's child. He set me free from all the lies about trying to win God's approval. I learned the truth, and it set me free.

Prayer:

Father God, thank You for sending Jesus. Show me how to find my identity in Him. Help me to recognize the lies I'm believing about myself. Thank You that I can look to your Word for the truth. I am not deceived, but I know who I am in Christ. In Jesus' name. Amen.

9

Make these declarations this week aloud. Believe them.

The truth is: "I am the righteousness of God in Christ Jesus" (*New International Version*,

2 Cor. 5.21).

"I am redeemed from the curse of the law" (*New International Version*, Gal. 3.13).

"I am a child of God" (*New International Version*, Rom. 8.15-16).

"I can go before God in prayer in time of need" (*New International Version*, Hebrews 4.16).

"I am fearfully and wonderfully made" (*New International Version*, Ps.139.14).

"It is not I who live, but Christ lives in me" (*New International Version*, Gal. 2.20).

The Word Brings Life

Read John 6:60-65.

"The Spirit gives life; the flesh counts for nothing. The words I have spoken to you—they are full of the Spirit and life" (*New International Version*, John 6.63).

Toddlers are so full of life. They have all this energy. When my grandkids were small toddlers, we had lots of toys in the house. I remember bringing a small plastic slide and a teeter-totter in the house for them to play. They loved it. They would play on it for a long time. Another thing they would do is run. I would count ready, set, go, and they would take off running to the door and back. Toddlers have so much life and energy that they don't even want to stop to eat or nap.

God's Word, the Bible, is full of the Spirit and life. A full life in Christ is an abundant life. When I am weak, His Word says that He is strong. When I think I can't do it, His word says I can do all things through Christ which strengthens me. When I am worried, He is my peace. In trouble, He is my refuge and strength. Reading His Word, meditating on His Word, and speaking His Word is powerful. The Bible is like a double-edged sword. It is alive, active, and cuts to the bone. Speak the Word in your situation. Speak life to broken relationships. Speak life to broken dreams. Speak healing to broken hearts; speak the Word and believe it produces faith.

Prayer:

Lord God, may I be aware of the words that I speak. May they produce good and be positive, aligning with your Word. May my words be full of life. I want to learn Your word to keep my mind on the good, the lovely, the excellent, and the praiseworthy. I ask in Jesus' name. Amen.

Courage

Read John 20:19-23; Acts 2.

"Everyone was filled with awe at the many wonders and signs performed by the apostles" (*New International Version*, Acts 2.43).

What a big difference between the disciples before and after being filled with the Holy Spirit! Before being filled, they were cowering, hiding, and afraid. However, in Acts, after they were filled, they are very bold. They went from ordinary, cowardly disciples to fearless apostles.

What can dramatically change a person like that? Only God! When Jesus left this earth, He sent the Holy Spirit to dwell in us, so we can have the power of God within us. When Christ walked the earth He couldn't be everywhere, but now the Holy Spirit can be everywhere. When we invite Him into our lives, He fills us up. We are never alone. He is our wisdom, guide, power, strength, courage, teacher, and comfort. Do you need those things? Then invite the Holy Spirit in your life today.

Prayer:

Holy Spirit, come into my life. Fill me up with the power, strength, wisdom, and courage. Make me bold, just as the disciples were in Acts. I want to live an abundant life here on earth. I ask in Jesus' name. Amen.

Shine Your Light

Read Acts 3:1-10.

"Then Peter said, 'Silver or gold I do not have, but what I do have I give you'" (*New International Version*, Acts 3.6).

My church went to the park to have an afternoon fellowship. While I was there, I was able to speak to a young mother that was not from my church. We exchanged small talk then I invited her and her two children to come to eat with us. She readily joined us. My church family extended such love towards her and her children. They enjoyed the popsicles and cookies. Later, I invited her to church and told her about our great children's ministry.

It didn't take a sermon to witness to her. Today, it was just a friendly conversation and sharing dessert. It felt good to reach out to someone. I could have said more. I could have tried to question her religious beliefs, but what I did was exactly the right thing. I planted spiritual seeds as I reached out to her, offered friendly conversation, and food. Now I will leave it in God's hands.

What does God want you to do today? Who does he want you to reach? What do you have to offer? You don't have to preach a sermon to reach out to others. Pray for divine appointments and God's wisdom as you go about your day.

Prayer:

Lord God, I want to be a light shining where You want, going where You want, saying what You want, and doing what You want. Help me to speak boldly about Jesus and for others to receive the message of Christ. In Jesus' name I pray. Amen.

Send Me

Read Matthew 2:1-10; Mark 16:15-20.

"Then I heard the voice of the Lord saying, 'Whom shall I send? And who will go for us?' And I said, 'Here am I. Send me!'" (*New International Version*, Isaiah 6.8).

At the age of thirteen, I didn't quite understand the full measure of my salvation. To tell the truth, I was trying to be like everyone else who had gotten saved at a much earlier age. In my teens, I was really drawn to God through Sunday School, our youth group, and my first taste of contemporary Christian music. There was such a pulling on my heart.

Throughout the next ten years, I kept feeling drawn to God but didn't know how to get more of God. I went up to rededicate my life almost every revival we had. I went to church, but nothing met that need. Finally, I was invited to a Spirit-filled Bible study and got filled with the Holy Spirit. That made the difference in my life. After that, I was excited about God, prayer, and His Word. I started to see things in a different way. It's like I had been blind, and after being filled with the Holy Spirit, I saw things differently and thought differently. I felt the peace of God more than ever.

In Matthew, the angel was saying you know the truth. You have been with Jesus. You've had that personal experience that others haven't-now go tell them about it. Go and share your experience, so others may know the salvation and peace of God. Tell them He has risen for them. That's what God wants us to do. Go and tell!

Prayer:

Lord, thank you for my salvation and the personal relationship that I have with You. Help me to share my witness with others. May I go and tell others whenever I have the chance. Here I am, Lord, send me. In Jesus' name I pray. Amen.

Imparting Wisdom

Read Proverbs 3:13-19.

"Where there is no guidance, the people fall, but in abundance of counselors there is victory" (*New International Version,* Proverbs 11.14).

"Let us not lose heart in doing good, for in due time we will reap if we do not grow weary" (*New International Version,* Galatians 6.7).

In high school, I sewed an outfit in Home Economics class. It was a flowered patterned crop top with lace at the bottom and with a high waist pink pants that belled out. I think they called them elephant pants. It sounds hideous now, but at the time it was groovy! It was quite an accomplishment for me to create it because I am not talented in that area.

Instructing us how to use the sewing machine and all that involves sewing actual wearable clothing was time-consuming for the teacher. Each day we continued our sewing project. What I remember most is that I needed a tremendous amount of her time and help. Every little step of the way, I needed more individual instruction and guidance. I was the worst sewer in my class! But the patient teacher would always come over to show me the next step. Until one day I had a completed project- a wearable work of art! My project was so cute that even my mom borrowed it and wore it.

What I remember most is that the teacher took so much of her time to help me. As I look back, I am grateful that the teacher was so nice to me and didn't give up. Because of her, I was able to finish a challenging project and look "Outta sight!"

Older men and women are supposed to help others giving them instruction, guidance, and imparting wisdom into young people. There is a lack of positive role models in the world today. Older Christians are called to be role models and lead the younger generation into God's callings. Like my high school teacher, exercise patience while instructing. We have already experienced situations in life that they are experiencing now or will experience in the future. Young people should take advantage of adults' wisdom. Use your interests and talents to bridge the generation gap. Is there someone that you can spend quality time with today?

Prayer:

Dear Heavenly Father, bridge the gap between the generations. May the generations be united not divided. Help me to see ways to spend time with others younger or older than me. Show me now if there is anyone you have in mind with whom you want me to form a stronger relationship. Help me contribute to others' lives and help me to find others to contribute to my life. May I not be too busy or impatient. May I see the impact these relationships can have in my life and theirs. In Jesus' name I pray. Amen.

God's Strength

Read Corinthians 12.

"Each time he said, 'No. But I am with you; that is all you need. My power shows up best in weak people.' Now I am glad to boast about how weak I am; I am glad to be a living demonstration of Christ's power, instead of showing off my own power and abilities" (*TLB*, 2 Corinthians 12.9).

For ten years I was the puppet director at my church. There is a certain way to manipulate puppets so the team had to practice doing it correctly. We always had to make the puppets move with our hand. Thank God we are not puppets. We can make our own choices. God gives us the freedom to make our choices whether they are good or not. We are not God's puppets but God's children.

When we allow God to use us then He is getting the credit, not us. He chooses imperfect humans to do his will, not puppets. When we are weak, He is strong in us. That is why I can do all things through Christ which strengthens me!

Prayer:

Dear Heavenly Father, thank you for the power and strength that you give me when I am weak. Your grace is sufficient for me. Thank you. Amen

Chapter 3: Hearing God's Voice

Peace

Read John 14:1-5; 25-31.

"Peace I leave with you; My peace I give to you; not as the world gives do I give to you. Do not let your heart be troubled, nor let it be fearful" (*New International Version*, John 14.27).

When my Aunt left this earth, I know that she was in God's embrace. During her last hours, most of the family was at her side. When she took her last breath, the family drew near and prayed; then we all sang, "Amazing Grace" and "I'll Fly Away." It was peaceful. Afterwards, love was poured out in hugs and embraces to comfort one another. That's what I want when I go to my heavenly home-faith, family, love, and peace.

In John 14:1, Jesus said, "Let not your heart be troubled" (*New International Version*). This scripture is often read at funerals. It can be comforting to those who know the Lord. My Aunt was a faithful believer and servant of God. My heart rejoices because I know she is in Heaven. Life is uncertain. Don't wait to make the decision to follow the Lord. Now is the time to dedicate or rededicate your life to God.

Prayer:
Dear God, thank you for your peace. Knowing Jesus can bring peace in what could be stressful situations. Thank you that You bring peace to those that know you and love you. When we believe that Jesus Christ is the Son of God and that He died on the cross and rose again, we can have peace that passes all understanding. Please bring others that to the knowledge of God's grace and peace. In Jesus' name. Amen.

The Father is Calling

Read 1 Samuel 16.

"For we are God's [own] handiwork (His workmanship), recreated in Christ Jesus, [born anew] that we may do those good works which God predestined (planned beforehand) for us [taking paths which He prepared ahead of time], that we should walk in them [living the good life which He prearranged and made ready for us to live]" (*Amplified Bible,* Ephesians 2.10).

When I was young, my little town had an 8:30 PM curfew for children 18 and under. At the exact time every night during the week, the siren would go off so all the kids would know to go home or get off the streets. The sound was distinct, loud, and calling us home. Most of us obeyed the siren.

At other times when I was playing somewhere in the neighborhood, my dad would whistle to call us home. I knew when I heard that whistle that I should be starting home. (This was way before cell phones.) That whistle was calling me; it was calling me home either for the night or for dinner. It was a distinct sound that could be heard all throughout the neighborhood. Everyone knew it was my dad, too. If we didn't hear it but someone else did, they would tell us. The neighbor's mom would say, "I heard your dad whistle. Time for supper." No matter where we were, my sister and I would stop what we were doing and start for home because our dad was calling us. We wanted to obey him. We wanted to please our father. We didn't want to get into trouble.

Our earthly Father calls us, watches over us, and loves us, even now our Heavenly Father is calling us. He is calling some to come to know Jesus as Savior. He is calling His sheep to do His will, to serve Him, and to use our talents for Him. We have a calling that is distinct, much like our personality. God has chosen you! He loves you and wants the best for you. Are you obeying? Do you hear His call?

Prayer:

My Dear Heavenly Father, thank you that You have chosen me and have called me. You knew me before I was born. Doing Your will and serving You shows my love for You. Help me to walk on the path You have chosen for me and obey my calling. May others hear you calling them to salvation. May they come to know Jesus as their Lord and Savior. In Jesus' name I pray. Amen

Speak, Lord

Read 1 Samuel 3.

And Samuel said, "Speak, for Your servant hears" (*New International Version,* 1 Samuel 3.10).

My sheep hear My voice, and I know them, and they follow Me (*New International Version,* John 10.27).

When I taught school I sometimes I has trouble hearing. Noise from other students or the heater often drowns out a soft voice in my classroom. If my ears are clogged up, I have a hard time distinguishing the exact words that are said, so I find myself asking them to repeat what they said. I have to really focus to hear a soft-spoken person sometimes. A clearer, deeper voice I can hear more easily.

Hearing God can sometimes feel like that. There is so much else swirling around in my head that it's hard to distinguish His voice. Often other things drown out His voice. To really hear God, I have to concentrate. Most of the time His voice is hard to hear, but I am practicing hearing God so it will become easier. Each day I pray for God to use me. In order to know what He desires me to do, it's necessary that I hear Him. Hearing His voice is vital in knowing His will.

When God called Samuel, he thought it was Eli. Three times God called Samuel before Eli instructed him to just listen because it was the Lord speaking. It was the first time that God had spoken to the young boy. When Samuel finally realized that it was God speaking to him, he listened carefully. Samuel wasn't used to hearing God. He had to learn how to distinguish God's voice from the priest's voice.

It may take some fine-tuning and practice to hear God and distinguish his voice from your own thoughts, but it can be done. God spoke to Samuel, and he still speaks to his children today. We don't have to be a prophet to hear God. He wants to instruct us, lead us, and encourage us. A good place to start is to pray and ask God to speak to you.

Another thing to do is get out your Bible, paper, and a pen so that you are ready to hear God as you read scripture. Write down what He says. Sometimes just turning off outside noise and distractions can help. Practice hearing His voice because with practice it will get easier.

Prayer:

Lord God, Your Word says that we are Your sheep, and You are The Shepherd. It says that we hear Your voice and do not turn to another. I want to hear Your voice clearly! I want to know without a shadow of a doubt that it is You when You speak. Help me to distinguish Your voice from my own thoughts or the enemy's lies. Fine tune my hearing. Speak to me, Lord, I am listening. In Jesus' name, I ask. Amen.

Too Busy

Read 1 Samuel 3.

So Eli told Samuel, "Go and lie down, and if he calls you, say, 'Speak, LORD, for your servant is listening.'" So Samuel went and lay down in his place (*New International Version*, 1 Samuel 3.9).

Even though my husband and I are empty nesters, I am still a busy person. Like most people, I am often too busy. There is a huge difference in my day when I start with prayer and study of the Word rather than a rushed morning when I miss spending time with God. There is also a big difference when I am in the Word, around Christian friends, and listening to worship music rather than filling my time with other things.

Like Samuel, when we get quiet or tune in to the Holy Spirit, we will hear what to do or be encouraged. God will speak to us. He may not speak audibly to us, but He often speaks to me when I read my Bible. As I read the Bible, I get thoughts about how it applies to something in my life. It often instructs me how to live or encourages me that God loves me and is faithful to me in the midst of difficult situations. I love these life lessons.

When Samuel was just three years old, his mother dedicated him to the Lord. He went to live with the temple priest, Eli. Eli trained Samuel how to serve the Lord.

Around age twelve, many years after coming to the temple, God spoke to Samuel. Thinking it was Eli calling him, he ran to him. Eventually, he discovered, through the advice of Eli that God was speaking to him. Take time, slow down, and tune in to hear what God is saying to you specifically. When we get quiet before God, we will find out that He wants to speak to us just like Samuel did.

Prayer:

Heavenly Father, thank You that You still speak to Your children even today. Speak to me and instruct me in Your truth. May I take time to really hear You. Help me to slow down to hear what You are saying to me. Speak Lord, Your servant is listening. I pray in Jesus' name. Amen.

Be Still

Read 1 Samuel 3.

"Be still and know that I am God" (*New International Version,* Psalm 46.10).

One beautiful fall evening, I saw a young couple walking down the street pushing a baby stroller. What a lovely sight to see! It made me miss those days when my children were young. As they got closer to me, I noticed that they were both on their phones, not texting, but talking on their phones at the same time! They were both distracted. How could they enjoy the walk, nature, their spouse, or their child? How ironic!

I see it often-people distracted by phones, texting, social media, television, work, etc. Too many things try to get our attention in our busy lives. I even find myself distracted by my phone or computer when I should be engaged in a conversation with my spouse. I noticed that the radio distracts me sometimes because it fills up the quiet with noise. Even in the car, if I'm not careful I will find myself ignoring others to listen to the radio or even my own thoughts. Turning the radio off helps me to carry on a conversation with others because I can focus on them. When I take that time to talk and listen, they often tell me things that I would have missed otherwise.

When I really want to hear God, I have to pay attention. I have to be quiet before God and not keep talking. It is like that old saying, "We have two ears and one mouth, so we should listen twice as much as we talk." This holds true even with God!

Prayer:

Heavenly Father God, I am so grateful that you want a relationship with your children. You want to speak to us. Lord, speak to me. May I know Your voice and not turn to another. Thank you, Holy Spirit that you are leading and guiding me. In Jesus' name. Amen.

Meditate on Him

Read Psalm 119.

"Open my eyes to see wonderful things in your Word. I am but a pilgrim here on earth: how I need a map—and your commands are my chart and guide. I long for your instructions more than I can tell" (*Living Bible*, Psalm 119.18-20).

When I was a teenager, I loved writing poetry. Listening to music inspired me to write. I would spend hours just writing my thoughts and feelings in a notebook filling them up with poetry. I've always kept a journal or a notebook full of my prayer requests, praise reports, and notes that I have taken while reading and studying my Bible or during sermons.

Journaling is encouraging to me because I can look back to see how God has answered my prayers. I can look back on the revelation that I received while studying the Word. I can read what God has spoken to me. Today I turn many of those thoughts into the devotions that I write and prayers that I pray.

Billy Graham's daughter told a class that I attended how her mother, the mom of four young children at the time, would carve out time in the Word by always having her Bible, notebook, and pen out on the table in the dining room. She would often see her mom stop to read, write something down, or pray throughout the day. This motivated me to start getting up early to spend time with God even though I am not a morning person. Spending this time at the beginning of my day is so important. It has really changed my day and me.

Take time to read, study, pray, and meditate on the Scripture. Have a pen and paper handy to write down what God speaks to you. Pray for God to speak to you.

Prayer:

Dear Heavenly Father, help me to be more disciplined in my quiet time. I want to establish a time to sit at Your feet and learn more of You through Your Word. I thank You that You still speak to Your children today. Help me to hear Your voice when I meditate on Your Word. May the scripture come alive in me. Open my eyes to see wonderful things in Your word. I want to hear Your voice today. I pray in Jesus' name. Amen.

Listen to the Word

Read Proverbs 3:5-6; John 10:26-30.

"Do not merely listen to the word, and so deceive yourselves. Do what it says" (*New International Version*, James 1.22).

When I was little, I remember my family and I always had unique cars, usually old ones. One car was a red 1963 Renault. It looked like a box because it was so small. Pushing it was the only way to start it sometimes. We would all be in the car, and my dad would get out and push it from the driver's side. Then, he would jump in the car quickly and off we'd go. When we went to Grandma's house, he'd park in the front on the street because it was on a hill. He could just roll down the hill in neutral to start it. It took some effort to get the car going at times, but once we got it going, it ran fine.

It took some effort to get the car started just like it takes an effort to spend time with God and to do His will. As Christians, we have to work on our relationship with God. We have to take the time to pray, study, meditate, and worship Him. We have to take the time to hear God and do what He says. No one said it would be easy. That's why we need practice. I try to hear God and do what He says, so I will get used to hearing His voice and acting on it. I try to discern what He is saying to me, so I can accomplish His will. God knows the bigger picture. He's at work in ways we don't see; we have to trust Him. We can't try to make things happen or rely on our own thoughts and ways. Trust God and do what He says.

I learned that the hard way through the years that my ways are definitely not God's ways. He has a master plan. I would much rather stick to His plan rather than my own. That is why I want to hear Him clearly. Hearing Him clearly will ensure that I am on the right path. Then, He will be able to use me for His kingdom. Let's work at hearing God and doing His will.

Prayer:

Father God, thank You that Your sheep hear Your voice. I am one of Your sheep, so I hear Your voice. Help me hear it clearly. Help me to not only hear it but to be quick to obey. I want to hear Your voice and follow Your plan for my life. In Jesus' precious name. Amen.

Know Him

Read Mark 4:35-41.

"He says, 'Be still, and know that I am God; I will be exalted among the nations, I will be exalted in the earth'" (*New International Version*, Psalms 46.10).

Busyness has overtaken our lives. We live in such a fast-paced world-fast food, texting, 70 mph speed limits, and deadlines. Go, go, go! Run, run, run! I'm not sure any of us take time like we should to really enjoy life. Are we happy with all the running around? Are we too busy? Why? Are our kids too busy with activities besides school?

I find that sometimes I am so focused on the next activity that I don't enjoy the present activity. In Psalms 46:10 the scripture says, "Be still and know that I am God" (*New International Version*).

Let's slow down. Take some quiet time with God, and enjoy our life! Are you too busy? Doesn't that just bring added stress to your life? Do we ever take time to enjoy our lives, our homes, and our families? Stop the merry-go-round that we are on so we can enjoy life.

Prayer:
Lord God, forgive me for the busyness that consumes my day. Help me to slow down. I want to make the right decisions for my family that will focus on what You want us to do. Help me to find my purpose each day. Help me to be still in Your presence so I will be refreshed and guided by Your Word. I pray in Jesus' name. Amen.

Fasting

Read Acts 13:1-4.

"Ask and keep on asking and it will be given to you; seek and keep on seeking and you will find; knock and keep on knocking and the door will be opened to you" (*New International Version,* Matthew 7.7).

I used to drink sweet tea from the time I woke up until the time I went to bed. I carried a glass around with me in the car or around the house full of that delicious drink all the time. Not understanding what all the alcohol commercials meant at the time, my youngest daughter told me in all seriousness that I shouldn't drink and drive. My best friend told me I was addicted, but I didn't believe her. Looking back though, I think I was addicted to iced tea and all that sugar.

My church calls a fast at least once during the year. I understand that you aren't fasting to twist God's arm to do something for you but fasting to really hear God so you can pray more effectively.

Sometimes I fast sweets, breakfast or lunch, TV, or reading the newspaper which isn't too hard except on a forty day fast. Once I felt compelled to fast my favorite addiction-sweet tea. I quit drinking it. When the fast was finished, I decided if I could stop drinking tea and soda for a short time then I could just stop drinking it altogether. I stopped once and for all, and that was years ago.

According to Andrew Bonar, "Fasting is abstaining from anything that hinders prayer." Fasting is taking time off from doing an activity like eating, watching TV, playing video games, or drinking tea to seek God more. It's making time to get in His presence more than usual. Fasting doesn't change circumstances or situations; it changes you. You may need direction or to hear a word from God. By getting quiet before Him during prayer and fasting, you will hear Him more clearly.

For me, it makes prayer more intense! I feel supercharged with confidence and boldness as I pray. Faith rises up in me when I really fast something that is a sacrifice.

Professor of Theology and Author, Williams Thrasher, agrees: "The abstinence is not to be an end in itself but rather for the purpose of being separated to the Lord and to concentrate on godliness. This kind of fasting reduces the influence of our self-will and invites the Holy Spirit to do a more intense work in us" (Williams).

Try a fast. Instead of eating or doing a certain activity use that time to study scripture, pray, worship God, seek Him, and you will definitely find him.

Prayer:

My Lord God in Heaven, show me what is stealing my time and reveal to me if there is anything You want me to fast. Help me during my fast to really seek You. I know if I do seek You, I will find You. May I not be distracted from praying. Help me to put You first in my life. I pray in Jesus' name. Amen.

Chapter 4: Trusting God

Trust Him

Read Hebrews 11.

"Trust in the Lord with all your heart and lean not on your own understanding; in all your ways submit to him, and he will make your paths straight" (*New International Version*, Proverbs 3.5-6a).

I think of all the people in the Bible who were called by God. They did so many great things! The early disciples walked in faith and supernatural power! Thousands were saved daily in Acts. Moses led the Israelites out of captivity to the Promised Land. Esther saved a nation of people. Solomon built the temple of God. Noah built an ark that saved his entire family and two of every animal to replenish the earth. Joseph was sold into slavery but rose to power that enabled him to save his family, including the brothers who sold him. David, a shepherd boy, defeated a giant and later became the king of Israel. He was even part of the lineage of Christ. What a legacy!

When I read about all the great accomplishments, it makes me wonder what I have accomplished? What will I accomplish for God? We can live life for ourselves, or we can go after God. Most people just live a random life going wherever life takes them rather than knowing that they are called for a purpose. When we trust Him, He directs our path; He guides our footsteps. He helps us make the right choices. Then we will take the right path that we are called to take. We have to not only trust God, but hear and obey Him. It all goes hand in hand.

If you are wondering what you are called to do, the first step is to follow after God. Next, let your life please Him in everything you do. Why not give it a try and see the supernatural, abundant life that He gives you!

Prayer:

Father God, thank You that I have been called out of darkness, death, hell, and the grave into life with You. I submit to You; I chose to live for You. Help me to trust You and to live for You each and every day. Help me to hear You clearly, obey quickly, and see You show up supernaturally wherever I go. May my life bring You glory. I ask in Jesus' name. Amen.

Overflowing Leftovers

Read John 6:1-15.

"And my God will meet all your needs according to the riches of his glory in Christ Jesus" (*New International Version*, Philippians 4.19).

From barely enough for a small boy to overflowing leftovers! That's our God. He takes the little or nothing and multiplies it. He takes the ordinary and moves through it to do the extraordinary! What seems barely enough, He blesses! What seems like a rough storm, He calms! What seems inevitable, He changes! What seems too big, too hard, or too much, He takes you through it! We aren't alone; God is with us!

One time when we were in a financial crunch waiting on the next payday that was not going to be soon enough, God intervened. Payday was far away, and we needed groceries and gas money. Unexpectedly, I got not one but five checks in the mail on the same day from my insurance because of overpayment. I had overpaid my copay about six months earlier when I had been to a new doctor several times. We ended up getting almost one hundred dollars back. Praise God; it was more than enough at the right time to buy groceries and gas. God is always faithful.

Prayer:

Heavenly Father, I thank You for always being there for my family. Thank You for helping us through difficult situations. Thank You for Your provision. Thank You for Your mercy and grace, but most of all, thank You for Your love for me. In Jesus' name I pray. Amen.

God Intervenes

Read Genesis 14:11-16; 18:16-32; 19:1-29.

"So when God destroyed the cities of the plain, he remembered Abraham, and he brought Lot out of the catastrophe that overthrew the cities where Lot had lived" (*New International Version*, Genesis 19.29).

I was heartbroken and crying because my boyfriend had broken up with me. My mom tried to console me, but it just irritated me. She said he wasn't good enough for me. I yelled at her, "I hate you!" and stormed off. What an awful thing to say to my mother! I look back now and realize that she just wanted to console me. I didn't want her help because I was a fickle teenager with a broken heart.

We don't always appreciate what we have until we are older. As I've matured, I look back and see all the things my parents did for me because they love me. God is the same way. He intervenes in our life. He is always at work even when we don't see him.

After reading about Abraham and Lot, I noticed that Lot didn't realize the impact that Abraham's prayers were having on his life. Abraham's prayers saved him. Lot could have chosen to stay in Sodom. He could have complained and stayed behind; instead, he listened to his uncle Abraham, and he was saved.

Prayer:
Lord God, Thank You that You send people to intervene in our lives through prayer and advice. I appreciate the

people that stand with me in faith. Thank You for all that my parents did through the years to help me and encourage me. Help me to pray like Abraham for my family and to be there for them. I pray in Jesus' name. Amen.

With Love

Read 2 Corinthians 9.

"You must each decide in your heart how much to give. And don't give reluctantly or in response to pressure. For God loves a person who gives cheerfully" (*New International Version*, 2 Corinthians 9.7).

A leader at my church had called me into her office to tell me that I should go to Russia on a mission trip with a couple from the church. I would teach the church there how to lead Children's Church and Puppets. I just laughed. Never in a million years could I go to Russia. First, I could never get that kind of money. Second, my children were elementary age, on summer vacation, and who would watch them for two weeks while my husband worked. After ten years of teaching in Children's Church and directing the church puppet team, I had the experience but was it possible? For me it wasn't, but for God all things are possible!

The next thing I knew, I was going to Russia. My husband agreed that I should go, and he volunteered to take his vacation during those two weeks to be with the girls. Individuals from my church and my parent's church started giving me money towards the trip. I had great support, but I needed a huge amount of money. I didn't have the money to give much myself, but everyone helped me. My neighbors and friends from the local church helped me by selling handmade items and even helped me cut out over five hundred flannel graph Bible characters from the two sets that my church was giving the Russian church. A Puppet business sent me four free puppets and several Russian puppet skits on tape. Our Children's Church bought many different items to use for object lessons. I got a foldable puppet stage and all kinds of fun prizes and gifts for children. Things were all coming together.

Two weeks before the trip, I still lacked two hundred dollars, but God came through. He made it happen, but he used people! Generous givers! Generous people! My supportive family, church family, neighbors, and friends! It was an experience of a lifetime! What I will never forget is the outpouring of love and generosity of others that made my trip possible! Thank God for people who give generously!

Prayer:

Dear Heavenly Father, please help me to be a cheerful giver, to live generously, and give when I see a need. Help me to be led by the Holy Spirit to pray, to give an encouraging word, a helpful hand, needed items, or even money. Just as others have generously given to me, let me help others in their time of need. I pray in Jesus' name. Amen.

Good Attitude

Read Philippians 1.

"Being confident of this, that he who began a good work in you will carry it on to completion until the day of Christ Jesus" (*New International Version*, Philippians 1.6).

For twenty years, my Grandma couldn't walk because of Rheumatoid Arthritis. The family started carrying her when it became too painful for her to walk. Her fingers and hands were all drawn up. She could barely lift a small glass of water. She sat in a comfy chair in the living room all the time, except when she took a nap in the afternoon or went to bed.

I took care of her for several years. My daughters would come with me and help me take care of her. I would make breakfast and lunch. The girls would take her orange juice to drink. One would bring her a straw. They would brush her hair. We would sit a chair right beside her, and the girls would sit next to great-grandma and show her their dolls. She would laugh and talk to them and hold their dolls.

The thing I remember most about her is her laughter. She was always saying little ditties like, "Love is love. Love is true. Who could keep from loving you!" Then she would laugh. I never heard her complain even though she was hard of hearing, couldn't walk, relied on everyone else to do things for her, and barely left the house, even the doctor made house calls.

They say laughter is the best medicine. Now studies are proving that is true. The Bible says the joy of the Lord is my strength. In Philippians, while Paul was in prison, he wrote the word joy or rejoice nineteen different times. Being in prison didn't get Paul down. Disabilities didn't get my grandmother down. My Grandma is my inspiration because she had a

41

fabulous attitude through adversity, just like Paul.

Prayer:

Dear Heavenly Father, may the trials of life not make me negative or discouraged or bitter but better. May I always have a good attitude and not complain. May I be content in all things like Paul. May I have the joy of the Lord. Thank You for strength and grace. I pray in Jesus' name. Amen.

God's Grace

Read 2 Corinthians 12:1-10; Philippians 4:13.

"But he said to me, 'My grace is sufficient for you, for my power is made perfect in weakness'" (*New International Version*, 2 Corinthians 12.9).

After being in a difficult labor and delivery for over 20 hours, my oldest daughter finally had a precious little girl. My first granddaughter was born half past midnight, but that wasn't the end of this night. I came out of her hospital room totally exhausted from the long day. I told my mom and my sister, "I can't do this again!" As they pushed me to the next hospital room where my youngest daughter was in labor, too. They said, "Yes, you can." Eleven hours later, my first grandson was born on the same day! What an exhausting, exhilarating two days! No sleep for forty-one hours! Not just one grandchild born that day but unexpectedly two grandchildren! What a great day to be a grandparent!

One baby was three days late, and the other baby was ten days early! We were expecting one labor and delivery that day, not two! Sometimes the unexpected happens, but God's grace is with us. We not only had God's grace, but we called it a Double Blessing!

Prayer:

Father God, when I go through difficult times, I know that You are with me. Send Your Holy Spirit to help me. When I am weak and ready to quit, help me. I can't do this on my own, but with You, I can do anything. Your grace is more than enough. Thank You for Your grace and blessings each day. I pray in Jesus' name. Amen.

Chapter 5: Following God's Will

God's Plan

Read Hebrews 11.

"'For I know the plans I have for you,' declares the Lord, 'plans to prosper you and not to harm you, plans to give you hope and a future'" (*New International Version*, Jeremiah 29.11).

Since I was a child, I wanted to be a teacher. I loved school! My sister and I played school with our school books during the summer. I was always the teacher because I was the oldest.

Throughout the years, I have taught Sunday School, Vacation Bible School, Children's Church, and in a public school. Teaching and learning is my passion and calling.

Noah, Jonah, Joseph, Mary, and Moses were some who were used by God. Everyone is called by God to do something! He has a plan and a purpose for your life. You just have to find out what it is. I've heard people say that they don't have any gifts, but that is not true. Some people work a regular job, but their ministry is singing at church or working in the nursery. Some people are generous, and God uses them to help others. Being a spouse or parent is the most important ministry. One thing I've learned is that you should use your gifts to serve God. Are you using your gifts?

Prayer:

Dear Father, I know that You have given me special gifts and talents to use. I pray that You lead me to use them in a way that pleases You. I know You have plans for my life. Help me to follow Your plan for my life. I ask this in Jesus' name. Amen.

Spring Break

Read Psalm 20:4-7; Proverbs 3:6; 16:9; 14:12.

"May he give you the desire of your heart and make all your plans succeed" (*New International Version*, Psalms 20.4).

Spring break! I looked forward to doing many home projects during my break this year like doing some painting, cleaning, shopping, and babysitting my grandkids. Before the break began, I prayed for God to help me make the right choices for the week. I would have liked to do certain things and even planned some things for certain days, but it didn't happen that way. I had to be flexible and not stress about the changes.

I needed to be productive here and there, to help out as needed, and clean when I had the time. It probably would irritate many people to hit and miss their plans, but I had to roll with it. I enjoyed the sunshine and the opportunity to do things at the spur of the moment. God wants our plans to succeed, but He'd like us to be in tune with His Spirit. Ask God what He wants You to accomplish each day and each week.

Prayer:

May all my plans be Your plans, Lord. May I not get off track but please guide my footsteps. Give me godly counsel from Your Word. May I be sensitive to the Holy Spirit so that I am always in Your will. I ask in Jesus' name. Amen.

Trail Run

Read Proverbs 3:5-6.

"Your word is a lamp for my feet, a light on my path" (*New International Version*, Psalms 119.105).

It was finally Saturday morning-Race Day! Five of us were going to run a two-mile charity run. Unbeknownst to us, it wasn't a regular race but a partial trail run. On trail runs you don't run on pavement but on a trail, so you have to watch your step because there may be roots, rocks, sticks, holes, ditches, mud, stumps, uneven ground, water, or a tree limb across the path. They are fun but not easy. You have to run slowly and be careful to get through it.

We took off at a fast pace down the sidewalk, but quickly the path veered off into the grass, around the pond, down a slight hill, across a ditch with water and mud in it, behind the ball diamonds, and through the gravel parking lot until we were on the road. Thankfully there were no mishaps, but a few times I had to slow down to jump the ditch and get out of the mud. I had to hold on to the ground getting up the slick incline and follow the runner in front of me to find the path because it wasn't marked clearly. I saw others fall, stumble, stop, or even walk during the race. Most runners wanted to get off the trail, so they could make up for lost time when they got to the road. That last quarter mile, we were home free! Paved roads are easier to run on because they are flat, empty, and free of any hindrances.

The trail run reminds me of life. It's not always easy. I often stumble or fall when I least expect it. It is full of hindrances, problems, and situations beyond my control. Sometimes I get off course, but I know that God loves me in spite of my mistakes or failures, and he forgives my sin. In the end, my goal is still the same, "Therefore, since we are surrounded by such a great cloud of witnesses, let us throw off everything that hinders and the sin that so easily entangles. And let us run with perseverance the race marked out for us, fixing our eyes on Jesus, the pioneer and perfecter of faith. For the joy set before him he endured the cross, scorning its shame, and sat down at the right hand of the throne of God. Consider him who endured such opposition from sinners, so that you will not grow weary and lose heart" (*New International Version*, Hebrews 12.2-3).

Prayer:

Father, forgive me for my sin. I thank You for the precious blood of Jesus that covers a multitude of sin. Thank You for Your love. Help me to stay on the path that You have laid out for me. Help me trust You and look to You when I encounter obstacles. In Jesus' name. Amen.

Obedience

Read Genesis 22; Romans 3:21-31; Romans 4.

What does Scripture say? "Abraham believed God, and it was credited to him as righteousness" (*New International Version,* Romans 4.3).

God tested Abraham. He told him to go sacrifice his beloved son, Isaac. God sacrificed His beloved son, Jesus. Abraham obeyed, just as Jesus obeyed. Abraham gathered up the supplies for a sacrifice and took his boy. In the same way, Jesus and the cross were taken to Calvary. Abraham told the servants to stay where they were, so they went on to worship God. What he said to them as he left was significant. He said, "We will come back to you." What faith! Isaac asked his father where the lamb was. "Abraham answered, 'God himself will provide'" (*New International Version,* Genesis 22.8). At the last minute, an angel of the Lord stopped Abraham from killing his son. God provided a lamb for Abraham; God has provided Jesus as a sacrificial lamb for us. Meditate on this passage this week.

Prayer:

Thank You, Lord, for Your Son and my redemption through Him. Help me to be more obedient to You. Increase my faith. I pray in Jesus' name. Amen.

Generosity

Read 2 Corinthians 9:6-9; Luke 6:38.

"The generous will prosper" (*New International Version,* Proverbs 11.25a).

My mom is such a giver. Most people, especially her family, recognize that she is a giver! She is so generous to her family, to a fault. She overdoes it! Every birthday, Christmas, Valentine's day, and Easter she spends countless hours and money on gifts for her entire family. We've tried telling her not to overdo it, but she continues because it gives her pleasure.

For example, at Easter, all the young grandkids and great-grandkids got an Easter basket from her and Papa which was packed full of presents. She also helped stuff the plastic eggs with gifts for an Easter egg hunt. I gave away cheese crackers, chocolate bunnies, candy, and fruit snacks with mine. She gave away money. The egg hunt was a huge success. My mom pours out her love by giving! She definitely has a talent! Her gift is giving and loving others! Generosity is a gift from God!

Every person has gifts and talents that God has given us. Each gift should be used to further the kingdom of God. I know my gift is teaching, because I taught in the public school district near me. I hope that I can positively influence students.

At church, I do different things to help others to know more about God. Sometimes I teach in Children's Church, teach an adult Sunday School class, or teach at Vacation Bible School. All this volunteering is to help others know God more and to help them have a closer walk with Him. Walking with God and doing His will is using my gifts for Him.

Prayer:

Dear Heavenly Father, thank you for the gifts and talents that You have given me. Help me to use them for good and to use them to further Your kingdom. Serving and helping others is part of Your commandments to love the Lord and to love others as myself. Show me how to be generous with my specific gifts You have given me, I pray in Jesus' name. Amen.

Grace and Courage

Read Esther 4:15-17; 1Samuel 16:1-13, 2 Samuel 5:1-5.

"When they saw the courage of Peter and John and realized that they were unschooled, ordinary men, they were astonished and they took note that these men had been with Jesus" (*New International Version*, Acts 3.13).

Courage is the "ability to do something that frightens one, strength in the face of pain or grief" ("courage"). Some things take courage to do. I often call it grace or anointing when a person does something that is not in his own strength. One can accomplish a task with God's help. This courage comes from God. After they were filled with the Holy Spirit, the disciples, who were once weak, then boldly spoke of their faith. That's how we know it's God: when the act is not accomplished by our own ability.

People think I am outgoing because I am a teacher, but I still feel shy at times, especially in a group of adults. There have been times though that I have taught adult Sunday School classes, given announcements at church, and even taught during the morning service. God helped me through because it wasn't a task that came naturally to me. He often takes ordinary people to do His will like when the shepherd boy, David, became King. The Jewish girl, Esther, became the Queen of Persia then saved her people. Joseph was promoted to a high place in the King's palace, so he was able to save his family when a drought came. God is looking for individuals who love Him and will serve Him no matter what He calls them to do or where He calls them to go. Can you say, "Here I am Lord, send me"? He will equip you when you accept the challenge or task.

Prayer:

Dear Father God, thank You that You not only call us to love

You but to serve You. It's exciting to see what I will do next for You. I'm always amazed at how You work through me since I am just an ordinary person. Thank You for Your grace. I pray in Jesus' name. Amen.

Following God's Will

Read Acts 13.

Therefore I urge you, brethren, by the mercies of God, to present your bodies a living and holy sacrifice, acceptable to God, which is your spiritual service of worship (*New International Version,* Romans 12.1).

As I was reading through Acts, I was thinking of a pastor and his wife. I thought of how Paul and Barnabas were sent to give the Good News to the Gentiles. They went about preaching the Word of the Lord. Many Gentiles received the Word and were saved and filled with the Holy Spirit. They had a specific calling on them. I feel this pastor and his wife had a specific calling on their lives. They were called from their home a few states away to go to a new church! It was their divine appointment. They packed up everything and left what was comfortable, left jobs, left their church, left their home, and left friends and family because God called them.

As I thought about it, I started thanking God for them, for their obedience, and for their love for God. They are a great example to the body of Christ because they got out of the boat and were led by God. And, they seemed happy and content to do it. Praise God.

Each of us is called by God. He has a divine purpose for you and for me. Before we were ever born, He knew us and loved us. We are His beloved children. All we do should glorify His name. Our daily lives, our behavior, words, actions, activities, and thoughts should bring praise to His name. That is our worship to God. So, as we accept the calling for our lives whether to go like the pastor and his wife or stay, it should glorify God. Walk in obedience, so you will be in God's divine will for your life.

"The events of our lives may appear to be random at times, but God is a master at arranging appointments at exactly the right moment. Behind every event, his divine hand is at work" (*NIV Once-A-Day Bible for Women*, 2 Kings 8.1-8).

Prayer:

Lord God, may I learn to walk in obedience to You. I want to hear You clearly and be willing to do Your will. Give me courage and strength to do what You call me to do. May I see each day as a new clean slate to serve You. Send divine appointments in my path. I pray in Jesus' name. Amen.

Walk on the Water

Read Matthew 14:22-33.

"Then Peter got down out of the boat, walked on the water and came toward Jesus" (*New International Version*, Matthew 14.29).

Recently I spoke at a Women's Retreat for my church. Speaking to a group of women was somewhat intimidating, but I prayed, planned, and studied the Word for weeks. I wrote things down that I thought I should say. Plus, I continued to study the book of Ruth. I felt God wanted me to use the verses in Ruth to encourage the women. Even with all the planning and time, I still wondered what God would do. Beforehand, I surrendered myself to God. I asked God to use me to say exactly what the women needed to hear and what He wanted to say through me.

I always find it amazing when God uses me. After all, who am I?! I am not an eloquent speaker, but God always shows up. It doesn't mean I'm not scared or worried. I was nervous at the retreat, but once I stepped in front of the women, I could feel God. I was amazed at how it flowed and even what I said. I felt empowered and anointed. I got out of the boat to do God's will and didn't let fear intimidate me.

When we read about Peter getting out of the boat, it seems like such a tremendous step of faith. Then, shortly after he stepped out, he took his eyes off of Jesus and almost drowned. We often speak about getting out of the boat as a sign of faith. We tell others or even ourselves to just get out of the boat. I think of it like it's doing God's will. If we have faith in God, we can do anything. When we obey God's call, we are walking in faith. We just have to recognize His voice, His command, and not take our eyes off of Him, so we aren't intimidated by our surroundings.

Obedience is vital to do God's will. If we let complacency, fear, or doubt keep us from getting out of the boat, then we limit what God can do through us. Be like Peter and get out of the boat of fear, complacency, doubt, or excuses; see what happens. Take a step of faith keeping your eyes on Jesus.

Prayer:

Dear Heavenly Father, thank You that You still speak to Your children today. I want to hear Your voice clearly, but I also want to be quick to obey. Help me to get out of the boat when you call me. May I do Your will as I continue to focus on You. In Jesus' name. Amen.

Protection in God's Will

Read Jonah.

"He who dwells in the secret place of the Most High Shall abide under the shadow of the Almighty. 2 I will say of the Lord, "He is my refuge and my fortress; My God, in Him I will trust" (*New International Version*, Psalm 91.1-2).

Even though I was ten years old, my Grandmother would still rock me. My toes would touch the ground each time she rocked, but I felt safe and loved in her arms. Sitting on her lap or getting a hug from her was like how a mother hen covers her babies with her wings. I felt all snug and protected. That's how I felt no matter what age I was! Her embrace felt as wonderful as sleeping in her feather bed, all warm, soft, safe, and comfy. Nothing felt as good as that bed and her hugs!

That's how it is when you stay in God's will. Obeying God will produce the best results for your life. He's like that Mother Hen wanting to protect us. God wants the best for us. I always think of His will as an umbrella. When we are in God's will, we are under the umbrella. Under that supernatural umbrella of the Holy Spirit, there is peace, joy, healing, safety, wisdom, guidance, provision, and comfort. However, when we walk by ourselves, away from God's will for our lives, we can get into a mess like Jonah did. He has a better plan for our lives if we just stay on His path. The path of life is set before you: God's way or your own way. Which will you choose?

Prayer:

Lord God, help me to walk in Your ways and follow Your path. Help me to hide Your Word in my heart, so I don't sin against You. Help me to see the path set out before me and walk obediently. Forgive me when I veer off the path on my own. Help me to get back on track quickly. It's not always easy to know Your will, so give me wisdom and discernment. I pray in Jesus' name. Amen.

Ultimate Obedience

Read Matthew 26:47-67; 27:11-65; 28.

"Surely he took up our pain and bore our suffering, yet we considered him punished by God, stricken by him, and afflicted. But he was pierced for our transgressions, he was crushed for our iniquities; the punishment that brought us peace was on him, and by his wounds we are healed" (*New International Version*, Isaiah 53.4-5).

Did you know that the calendar was created after the birth of Christ? Did you know that A.D. does NOT mean after the death of Christ? Teaching that to fifth graders every year for over 25 years has been frustrating! No matter how many times we discuss it, look it up, write it down, and study it, a few will still miss it. It really is confusing.

A.D. stands for the Latin words "anno domini" which means "the year of our Lord." The years of the calendar are all referring to Jesus' birth, either before or after. It's ironic that in a world where so many are trying to get rid of anything that has to do with God, our whole calendar system is based on the birth of our Lord Jesus!

As Christians, we know that His birth was a supernatural miracle. Jesus' death and resurrection was a supernatural miracle, too, especially when you realize that He chose to come to earth to be a sacrifice for mankind. Because of His obedience, Jesus was mocked, ridiculed, spit on, beaten, and hung on a cross. He was tortured. His love for you and I outweighed the pain of His death. His resurrection gives us hope and life if we believe.

Prayer:

Dear Father God, thank You for Your Son, Jesus. He is the light of the world. He is the bread of life. He was the sacrifice for all mankind. Thank You that You had a plan to reconcile us back to You. Thank You that I have come to know Jesus Christ as my Lord and Savior. Help me to be obedient in that which You call me. In Jesus' precious and holy name, I pray. Amen.

Deny Yourself

Read Acts 16:16-40.

"Then Jesus told his disciples, 'If anyone would come after me, let him deny himself and take up his cross and follow me. For whoever would save his life will lose it, but whoever loses his life for my sake will find it. For what will it profit a man if he gains the whole world and forfeits his soul? Or what shall a man give in return for his soul?'" (*New International Version,* Matthew 16.24-26).

My pastor was speaking about hearing and obeying God. Surrendering our will is the first step to obeying. He asked what if you get near the end of your life and find out that you only did God's will 20% of the time. That startling fact scared me. I have given my life over to God. I have surrendered, but I know that I still follow my flesh way too much.

Lately, God's been dealing with me about my evenings. After I get home or after dinner, I sit down to work on grading, lesson plans, studying, and writing. The next thing I know, I have checked my emails and social media. I have wasted thirty minutes or more and never started on my work. Sometimes, I turn on the TV as I work. Then I noticed that I have sat there way past the time it took to finish my work. Looking back at my evening, I noticed the amount of time that I have wasted. I should have been more productive Imagine what I could accomplish if I didn't get distracted!

Look at Paul, even in jail he accomplished so much. He wrote so many letters and books of the Bible. He told everyone about Jesus. He told the jailers about Jesus. He was a Jesus freak! It makes me ask myself if I am doing all that I can do to spread the gospel of Christ? I may not be walking from town to town or getting thrown in jail, but God does want me to surrender my talents for his kingdom. I can't preach on a street corner or be the next Billy Graham. However, I can use the gifts that God has given me. God has strategically placed me in my family, workplace, and church to be used by Him. Realizing that is my mission is an important part of doing God's will.

The Word says, "Take up your cross daily and follow me." It takes a daily surrender, a daily commitment to live your life for God. I don't want to look back on my life to see that I wasted 80% or more of it doing my own thing. How about you?!

Prayer:

Precious Father God, forgive me for not fully living for You. Help me to lay down my flesh and surrender daily to You. I truly desire to do Your will. Holy Spirit, fill me with courage to complete my mission. I pray in Jesus' name. Amen.

Temptation

Read Psalm 51.

"If we confess our sins, He is faithful and righteous to forgive us our sins and to cleanse us from all unrighteousness. If we say that we have not sinned, we make Him a liar and His word is not in us" (*New International Version*, I John 1.9-10).

A brownie in a clear package with nuts and icing was tempting me. I had walked to the small grocery store during lunch. In 6th grade they let us leave at lunchtime. Without thinking much about it, I grabbed a brownie off the shelf and stuffed it in my pocket. I stole a brownie. I don't really know why. It would have only cost me twenty cents. It was the worst tasting brownie I'd ever eaten. It was full of guilt and hard to swallow.

I wish I could say I never did anything wrong, but all too often I fail. The Bible says that we all sin and fall short of the glory of God. Isn't that an understatement! I'm so glad that God is faithful to forgive us of all our sins. All we have to do is confess. Jesus died on the cross for all our failure, sin, and childish mistakes.

We can't blame our sin on others or even God. I can't blame the factory for the clear wrapper that showed how delicious the brownie was or the store for not locking it up in a case. I can't blame my parents for not giving me money. I can't blame the school for letting me have such a long lunch break and permission to eat off campus. I can only blame myself. God doesn't tempt us, but our own fleshly, sinful desires do. Thankfully, God always gives us a way out.

My own experience with temptation is why I relate to David. He went through seasons of life just like me. There were times when he was afraid, elated, depressed, frustrated, prayerful, worshipful, and thankful. There were times when he messed up, made wrong decisions, sinned, and even tried to cover it up. He was a lowly shepherd, a loyal servant, glorified King, mighty warrior, yet a failure at times. His poor choices caused others harm, but God still described him as a man after His own heart. David continued to love God and pour his heart out to Him. Just read the Psalms. I am so glad that God is always faithful even when we are not!

Prayer:

Dear Heavenly Father, thank You for Your love. Forgive me of my sin and failure. Thank you for Your forgiveness. Walking in Your ways and pleasing You is what I want to do. Holy Spirit, give me discernment and power to overcome the temptations that come my way. Show me the way out that You are providing me in these times. In Jesus' name, I pray. Amen.

Fruit Bearing

Read John 15:1-16.

"I am the true vine, and my Father is the gardener. He cuts off every branch in me that bears no fruit, while every branch that does bear fruit he prunes so that it will be even more fruitful" (*New International Version,* John 15.1) .

"Remain in me, as I also remain in you. No branch can bear fruit by itself; it must remain in the vine. Neither can you bear fruit unless you remain in me" (*New International Version,* John 1.4).

We have a tulip tree in our front yard. The yard often looks like it rained sticks. There are sticks all over the ground-some large but most are small. They are sticks, not leaves. Of course, leaves fall off too. I was thinking about why a branch wouldn't stay on the vine. I see them on the ground a lot. When they fall off, they die because they aren't hooked to the life source. People fall away from God too. They go after different things that aren't life giving. Only being plugged into God is life-giving.

Why do branches fall? There is a storm or heavy rain that shakes them loose. Maybe the roots of the tree aren't deep, so the whole tree falls. Maybe the tree is injured or diseased, and it dies. Maybe it is a new branch that's not very sturdy, so it falls off. Compare yourself to the tree; are you spiritually healthy? Are you connected to the Source?

Unless Christians remain in Christ, we will have no good fruit. If we disconnect from God, our works are in vain. Sometimes when I feel stressed I know I need to plug into God. Spending time with God in worship, praise, prayer, or Bible study will strengthen and encourage me. When I do things on my own it's not fruitful. Being fruitful means to do

God's will.

"[Not in your own strength] for it is God Who is all the while effectually at work in you [energizing and creating in you the power and desire], both to will and to work for His good pleasure and satisfaction and delight" (*Amplified Bible,* Philippians 2.13).

Prayer:

Father God, help me to stay connected to You, to abide in You continually so that I can do Your will for Your good pleasure. Abiding in You will help me produce good fruit. May I continue to pray, worship, praise, and study my Bible each day so that I know Your will. In Jesus' name. Amen.

Return to the Father

Read Luke 15:11-32.

"For this son of mine was dead and is alive again; he was lost and is found" (*New International Version*, Luke 15.24).

When I was in my teens, like most teens, I thought I knew everything. Often, I ignored my parents' advice, thinking I knew better only to realize later I was wrong. Now I realize that my parents wanted to keep me from making mistakes or getting hurt. That's why they were always giving me unwanted advice. They were trying to keep me out of trouble and away from heartache and pain.

The younger immature son in Luke 15 wanted to go live the high life. It was his money, and he wanted it so he could waste it on unnecessary pleasures. Doing our own thing seems fun, but Proverbs 16:25 states, "There is a way that appears to be right, but in the end, it leads to death" (*New International Version*). I am sure the son was raised by a wise father, but the father said nothing because it was his son's inheritance. The Father doesn't interfere.

That's such a picture of God, our loving Father. He gives us free will to do what we want even if it's against His will. Often, we go down the wrong road thinking it's more fun, leaving our Father behind.

Are you doing God's will? If in doubt, pray and ask Him. Have you turned away from God to do your own thing? It's time to return to your Heavenly Father. He will welcome you with open arms. Pray for yourself or others in this situation.

Prayer:

Forgive me, God, for my selfish ways. I surrender to you. Help me to get my life back on track again. I want to be in Your will for my life. I ask in Jesus' name. Amen.

Chapter 6: Forgiveness

Healing

Read John 20:21-23; 1 Peter 5:7; Ephesians 4:32; 2 Corinthians 5:17-18.

"If we confess our sins, he is faithful and just to forgive us our sins and to cleanse us from all unrighteousness" (*New International Version*, 1 John 1.9).

It was the first time that I remember seeing my dad cry. After the emergency phone call, I had driven to the hospital to find my dad and aunt in a tiny room that was the chaplain's office. I remember being anxious as I walked into the room. Finding my dad and aunt crying told me for certain that my grandmother had passed away. I was twenty years old when my grandmother died unexpectedly, and I will never forget it.

Do you know what sticks in my mind? I hadn't seen her in two weeks. I had been so wrapped up in my own life that I didn't even know she was sick. I am not sure anyone else did either though. She didn't tell anyone until she had to go to the hospital, until it was too late.

Regret is an evil bully pushing its way into thoughts, bringing up the past, and causing pain for wrong choices we have made. It just beats you up in your mind. It bombards you with the what ifs. Yes, I know God forgives me, but it was hard to forgive myself. I made a mistake because I was too busy! Thank God for the precious memories of my grandmother and a future Heavenly reunion someday!

God doesn't want us bullied by guilt. He doesn't send condemnation. That is from the enemy of our soul. The best way to bring life into a situation is to forgive; whether it's yourself or someone else; forgiveness frees the soul.

Prayer:

Father God, although it's difficult, I give you all the pain, heartache, and regret that I am feeling. I chose this day to forgive myself. I know that Your love brings forgiveness. Thank You for Your healing balm and peace. Free me, so I can do the same for others, so I can be an agent of forgiveness. I pray in Jesus' name. Amen.

Measuring Up

Read Romans 5:1-8; Romans 8:14-16.

"But God demonstrates his own love for us in this: While we were still sinners, Christ died for us" (*New International Version*, Romans 5.8).

"The Spirit himself testifies with our spirit that we are God's children" (*New International Version*, Romans 8.16).

People often mistakenly think that they have to get their lives cleaned up before they can come to God. With God it is the opposite; He wants us to want Him to help us. If we could do it ourselves, we wouldn't need Him. What's unique about God is that He is a loving Father, and He looks beyond our mistakes, sin, and mess. He forgives our sin because of the sacrifice of His Son, Jesus. We don't have to measure up. Because of what Jesus did for us, we are forgiven. We don't have to perform or try to please God. It's hard to think that God loves us like a Father, but He does.

My coworker's twins got up during the night and played with the baby powder. When she went into their room the next morning she found a huge mess, but it didn't make her love her children any less. Although she had a huge mess to clean up, it didn't cause her to even think about loving them less or kicking them out of the family. She knows that children made mistakes like we all do.

God is the same way. What we do or don't do does not make Him love us any more or any less. Take the pressure off yourself, and quit trying to measure up. God loves you no matter what you do or don't do. He won't kick you out of His family just because you've made a mess of your life. With God, our mess can be cleaned up. God's love is everlasting. Ask God to forgive you. He is a forgiving Father. Invite Jesus into your heart and you will never regret it!

Prayer:

Dear Heavenly Father, thank You that I don't have to work to please You or make You love me. No matter what I have done, You still love me. You already love me because I am Your child. The love that You have shown me through the sacrifice of Your dear Son, Jesus, is more than enough. Thank you. I love You. In Jesus' name. Amen.

Rainbows are Promises

Read Genesis 9:1-17.

"I set My bow in the cloud, and it shall be for a sign of a covenant between Me and the earth" (*New International Version*, Genesis 9:13).

Imagine having only one route out of town because of flooding and that route is a very long way to everywhere else. Many roads were flooded back in 2011, which caused major travel problems. Of the four highways leading to our small town, only one was open. The river and creeks swollen with water flooded all the farmland for miles. Homes, churches, and some businesses in its path were flooded. One day, a few friends and I went down the closed road to see the water. It was an eerie sight to see water everywhere and such silence. Water was where it should not be. It was everywhere we looked for miles. It was all because of so much rain.

Now, imagine that you are Noah. God commands you to build an ark with very specific directions. He is going to flood the whole earth. Thank God that He has promised not to do that again. Don't you love to see a rainbow in the sky! God doesn't have to send another flood because He sent Jesus. Once for all, the price was paid. Jesus wiped our sins away with His sacrifice on the cross. God does not see our sin once we have accepted Jesus as our Lord and Savior. We are cleansed from all sin.

Prayer:

Father God, thank You for your promises. I'm so thankful for Jesus' sacrifice. You must love me very much to give Your only Son Jesus as a sacrifice for me. Thank You for Your love. I love You. In Jesus' name. Amen.

My Redeemer Lives

Read the book of Ruth.

"And Naomi said to her daughter-in-law, blessed be the name of the Lord who has not ceased his kindness to the living and to the dead. And Naomi said to her, the man is a near relative of ours, one who has the right to redeem us" (*Amplified Bible*, Ruth 2.20).

"Redeemed-How I Love to Proclaim it" was a hymn I used to sing all the time. For years, it was one of my favorites. Then Nicole C. Mullen wrote and sang "My Redeemer Lives." The words to this song became my song! The words touched my heart.

It reminds me of the book of Ruth. Naomi became a widow. Later, she lost her two sons, too. One of her daughters-in-law went back to live with her own family, but Ruth refused to leave her mother-in-law, Naomi. The two widows went back to Jerusalem together. Ruth gathered the left-over grain from a field. Then, they found out that the field belonged to a relative of Naomi's named Boaz. How wonderful to have the favor of the owner, but she had more than favor! They were related. In Ruth 2:20, Naomi states that he is a relative that can redeem us. He eventually does redeem them both. He marries Ruth, and she has a son.

A redeemer sets you free. He redeems you from your injustice or circumstances like in the book of Ruth. Just as Boaz redeemed Ruth and Naomi, Jesus redeemed us. He set us free by going to the cross to take our blame, our shame, and to clear us of our sin. He rescued us from darkness and sin. He delivered us from evil. He saved us from Hell. He paid the price to give us eternal life. I am so happy and thankful that my Redeemer set me free!

Prayer:

Dear Heavenly Father, Thank You for redeeming me from the curse of the law. Thank You for the sacrifice that Jesus paid on the cross for my sin. Thank You that I have been delivered, saved, rescued, and redeemed. May others hear the good news of what Jesus did and be saved, too. I pray in Jesus' name. Amen.

Chapter 7: Our Mission of Love

Love One Another

Read 1 John 4:7-8.

Jesus said, "A new command I give you: Love one another. As I have loved you, so you must love one another. By this everyone will know that you are my disciples, if you love one another" (*New International Version,* John 13.34-35).

After praying and reading the Word, I had an image of an old window in an old house. It was stuck. It had not been used for a very long time. The paint was peeling, and it was painted shut. It needed a good push or some scraping around the edges to open it. It was not useful because it was shut so tightly. It was not being used for its purpose. Also, the glass needed a thorough cleaning because you could not see through it. It was dim, cloudy, and foggy.

Sometimes, I feel like that old window. I am stuck in a rut and not being useful to God. I keep living life the same old way. My perspective is skewed because I have cloudy vision. I need to be refreshed, revived, and to become useful again. I need to be filled up with the Holy Spirit and my soul stirred up. I need to know my calling. My mission in life is not sitting around watching TV or doing all the activities I want to do. It is not about me; that is selfish. It is about what God wants me to do. Am I accomplishing my calling? Do I even realize what it is? Do I even care?

After seeing the image of the window in my mind, all of a sudden, I realized that I was the window. I am stuck, so I started praying for more opportunities. I started listening to a mission-minded preacher. I got more involved in really following the leading of the Holy Spirit. Now I am on the lookout for those divine appointments. Plus, I am praying that I truly love others as Jesus said. Will you join me on this mission? Will you start praying? Will you start going where He leads? Saying what He says? Doing what He says?

We cannot have a dim and cloudy vision. We need God to open our eyes to the opportunities around us.

Prayer:

God, forgive me for being selfish and too busy. Please pull me out of this rut. I do not want to be stuck. Revive me! Put a godly love in my heart for others. May I truly love You with all my heart, soul, mind, and strength, and then love others as myself. Show me how.

Holy Spirit, fill me up, so I can truly be used of God. Fine tune my hearing and sight, so I can go where You lead and do what You want. I pray in Jesus' name. Amen.

The Good Samaritan

Read Luke 10:25-37.

"'Which of these three do you think was a neighbor to the man who fell into the hands of robbers?' The expert in the law replied, 'The one who had mercy on him.' Jesus told him, 'Go and do likewise'" (*New International Version*, Luke 10.36-37).

When I helped teach in Children's Church, we had a Birthday Bank. If a child had a birthday sometime that week, they would bring in coins for how old they were to put in the bank. For example, when a child was seven, they would bring seven coins to put in the Birthday Bank. The children would count each coin out loud as it went in the bank. I still remember how excited they were to find out the age of the person especially if it was an adult. We would sing our special birthday song, try to guess the person's age, and then count the coins as they went in the bank. That money was used to sponsor a child in Africa through Compassion International.

Each month Children's Church made enough money from the offering to pay for a child in need to have food, clothing, and an education. Receiving letters and pictures from the child was so special to the children; they were always happy to give an offering. It made their giving real to them. They could see where their money was going. It made an impact on them. We all learned the value of giving.

Jesus wants us to give and help others in need. Whether it's physical, financial, or emotional, we should be like Jesus. Helping others in need may open the door for them to receive Jesus. The greatest need anyone has is to have a personal relationship with Jesus. Helping the physical need may open the door for you to witness to a person's spiritual need.

In Isaiah it says to fast by doing these things; "Is not this the kind of fasting I have chosen: to loose the chains of injustice

78

and untie the cords of the yoke, to set the oppressed free and break every yoke? Is it not to share your food with the hungry and to provide the poor wanderer with shelter—when you see the naked, to clothe them, and not to turn away from your own flesh and blood?" (*New International Version*, Isaiah 58.6-7). Walk in God's love and mercy this week like the Good Samaritan. Make a difference in someone's life.

Prayer:

Dear Lord God, help me to walk in Your love reaching others for Your kingdom. I want to see the need and have the means to help others. May I discern the ways to be a good neighbor to others in my life. May Your love and mercy flow out of me. I pray in Jesus' name. Amen.

Reaching the Lost

Read Isaiah 58.

"Is this not the fast that I have chosen: to loose the bonds of wickedness, to undo the heavy burdens, to let the oppressed go free, and that you break every yoke? Is it not to share your bread with the hungry, and that you bring to your house the poor who are cast out; when you see the naked, that you cover him, and not hide yourself from your own flesh?" (*New International Version,* Isaiah 58.6-7).

Last night I went to a concert. All the songs were beautiful, but one really touched my heart and intrigued me. It was a song that cried out to God to help the outcasts. It made me wonder who would sing that type of song. I found out that it was from the movie *The Hunchback of Notre Dame* titled "God Help the Outcasts." The main character, Esmeralda, sang this as a prayer to God in the cathedral, "God help the outcast, hungry from birth; show them the mercy they don't find on earth." As others were asking for wealth, love, glory, and fame, she sang, "I ask for nothing; I can get by, but I know so many less lucky than I. Please help my people the poor and downtrod. I thought we all were children of God."

Those lines from the song reminded me of the verses in Isaiah 58 about fasting. It says the correct fast that God wants us to do is to help others. We should reach the lost, the hungry, the afflicted, the suffering, the needy, and those in bondage; we should help the outcast, the overlooked, and the rejected. How does God help the outcasts on earth? He uses us. When we reach out with compassion and mercy, then God is using us. Remember we are His hands and feet on the earth. We are to bring Jesus to the lost. We are to show mercy and compassion like we have been shown by God, our Father.

The Message Bible says it like this, "What I'm interested in seeing you do is: sharing your food with the hungry, inviting the homeless poor into your homes, putting clothes on the shivering ill-clad, being available to your own families. Do this and the lights will turn on, and your lives will turn around at once. Your righteousness will pave your way. The GOD of glory will secure your passage. Then when you pray, GOD will answer. You'll call out for help and I'll say, 'Here I am."

Let's live like Jesus. Live Isaiah 58.

Prayer:

Lord God, help me to have eyes of compassion and mercy towards others. I often get caught up in my own little world, but I want to hear Your voice clearly to help others, to do Your will, to be generous and kind. Forgive me when I fail. Let me be like Jesus. Let others see Jesus in me. I pray in Jesus' name. Amen.

Thoughtful

Read Colossians 3:12; John 13:34.

"Little children, let us not love in word or talk but in deed and in truth" (*New International Version,* 1 John 3.18).

My aunt is such a sweet and thoughtful aunt! All my life, I remember always getting birthday, graduation, and Christmas cards and gifts from her. Now that I am grown, the cards and gifts from her keep coming. After my daughters were born, she started sending them cards and gifts as well. When my grandchildren were born, she made sure to send them a little something every year, too. She not only sends gifts, but she sends thoughtful gifts.

Every Christmas, she gets a large basket of goodies, cookies, or a huge box of candy for our entire family to share. I always love looking through the treasure to find special candies or tasty cookies. I cannot imagine all the time and money that she has used throughout the years to do this for our entire family, my siblings and their families, my children, and my grandchildren! Plus, she has a very large family of her own. When two of my grandchildren and a nephew just graduated, guess what? They all got cards and money from their great aunt! What a sweet and thoughtful lady!

A thoughtful gesture warms the heart and blesses us. Maybe we should be more kind towards others. Just like my aunt, we can brighten someone's day by showing them love. Let the Holy Spirit show you how to bless others, maybe even in unexpected ways! Let God use you!

Prayer:
Dear Heavenly Father, thank You for Your love. You created

love, and it is such a wonderful thing. Thank You for special people that show love to others. Let me be a loving person-compassionate and helpful to others. Help me to put away selfishness and walk in love. I pray in Jesus' name. Amen.

Be Nice

Read Luke 10:25-37.

"In the same way, let your light shine before others, that they may see your good deeds and glorify your Father in heaven" (*New International Version*, Matthew 5.16).

Today while I was driving, a lady gave me the middle finger! I was completely dumbfounded. What had I done that was so terrible to deserve that? I think that I am a nice person, so it really hurt my feelings.

Earlier I had been driving down a four-lane highway in town when I came to construction. The other lane was completely stopped and could not get over into my lane because of so much traffic. I slowed to let the first car out. You know when there is a slow traffic jam and others are merging and you let one car in every so often. Well, that's what I did. Then I kept on driving when suddenly a lady quickly pulled in front of me. Later, I tried to pass her as the lanes merged, but she would not let me. When she turned into the turn lane, I passed her, and she gave me the middle finger. I was shocked. I tried to figure out who the person was and what I had done to her.

That must have been the second car in the traffic jam in the construction area. I had let the first car out, and it didn't even cross my mind to let the second car out. It must have crossed her mind because she was very mad. It really surprised and hurt me! I had tried to be nice but apparently not nice enough.

It really made me think. Do I go out of my way to help others? I think being upset by her hateful gesture was just part of it. The other part is that I don't like people being mad at me and thinking I am mean.

Now I have determined to look for ways to be helpful

and kind to others. Isn't that how our light shines? If I really care for others, then I will show them that I care by my actions. It's like that saying "Actions speak louder than words."

Prayer:

Lord God, I want to be nice, helpful and kind to others. Help me to really care for others and to love them as you do. Show me creative ways to help them. Remind me to encourage others. I want to have the fruit of the Spirit, love, operating in my life more effectively. Let my actions speak louder than words. In Jesus' name, I pray. Amen.

Share

Read Isaiah 6:8; Philippians 2:20-21; Mark 16:15-18.

"But you will receive power when the Holy Spirit has come upon you; and you shall be My witnesses both in Jerusalem, and in all Judea and Samaria, and even to the remotest part of the earth" (*New International Version*, Acts 1.8).

You know how toddlers hate to share toys. They want it all for their own. When they play with a toy, they sometimes hang on to it so no one else will take it, even if they are at someone else's house or even at daycare. They do not know how to share. I noticed one boy who still wanted the toys all for his own even if he was not playing with it. It caused some problems because other children just saw a toy and did not realize that he had claimed it. It was like everything within his reach was his. He had a tight little circle of toys that he was keeping for himself.

This reminds me of our behavior before we come to know Christ and many times even after. We live in our little worlds of self-centeredness. It's all about me-my world, my family, my friends, and my job. We forget that we are put on this earth to share Jesus with others. We should not keep Him all to ourselves. The Good News is meant to be shared with others. Others need to know the freedom, the peace, and the joy that we have because of Him, so they can receive it, too. Let's not be like selfish children living just for ourselves; let's share the love of God with others.

We should be ready to share what God has done for and through us. When individuals go through difficult situations, we can share how God brought us through a similar situation. Tell how we rely on God. Another way to share God's love is to be there when someone is going through a hard time like praying for them, calling them, sending a short note or card, and encouraging them. Being in someone's life can be the avenue to tell them about Jesus.

Let's share our toys, our Jesus, our blessings, ourselves with others. Let's not be like a selfish child who hoards all the good things for himself. Spread out beyond your little circle of friends and family. Be ready to share Jesus with others.

Prayer:

Dear Almighty Father who made Heaven and Earth, thank You for Your great love for me. I am grateful and overwhelmed with the love and salvation that You have given me through Jesus Christ my Lord. May You give me opportunities to share Your love with others. Help me recognize those in need. Give me divine appointments. I don't want to be selfish and self-centered but to reach others with the good news of Christ. May I speak boldly and go obediently where You send me. I pray in Jesus name. Amen.

Helping Others

Read Matthew 25:31-46.

"Then the King will say to those on his right, 'Come, you who are blessed by my Father; take your inheritance, the kingdom prepared for you since the creation of the world. For I was hungry and you gave me something to eat, I was thirsty and you gave me something to drink, I was a stranger and you invited me in, I needed clothes and you clothed me, I was sick and you looked after me, I was in prison and you came to visit me" (*New International Version*, Matthew 25.34-36).

When my children were young, we did not have much money. For a time, we barely scraped by. My neighbor had two daughters, too. She often gave us a bag of clothing that her children had outgrown. It was like Christmas at my house when she did that. My daughters delighted in taking each piece out to look at it and try it on. They did not care that they were hand-me-downs. To them, it was new.

My neighbor was one of the most generous people I knew, besides my own mom. She would have given me the shirt off of her back if she thought I needed it. It was so appreciated and just as humbling to have someone give us so much, especially someone that was not family.

My family learned to appreciate all the things they received from others. It made us feel loved, and I felt God was taking care of us. Others' generosity towards my family and I turned me into a giver. Today when I change out my clothes during a change of seasons, I always have a huge bag of clothing and shoes that I either give away or give away. I remember how I felt when we could not afford much, but God used people to help us. I hope now I can help someone in need. May God use me to help others.

Prayer:

Father God, I am so thankful for how You provide for my family throughout the years. You placed special people in my life to help my family. Now may I be used to help others. Show me the need and how I can reach out. I pray in Jesus' name. Amen.

Love One Another

Read John 15:9-17.

"Greater love has no one than this: to lay down one's life for one's friends. This is my command: Love each other" (*New International Version*, John 15.13 &17).

There used to be a saying that was quite popular with Christians: "What would Jesus Do?". It was supposed to remind us that everything we do should glorify God. If we really followed that quote, it would help us to do God's will.

Laying down our lives and our own fleshly desires to live for God is exactly what He wants us to do! We should follow Jesus' example. He went about continually showing love to people. God loved us even while we were sinners. He loves those who hate him and those who do not believe in him. He wants all to be saved.

The greatest sacrifice anyone has ever made for you is Jesus. He died for all mankind whether we love Him or not. He died for you. He died for those who persecuted him, those that mocked him, and those that ridiculed him. Since he gave such a tremendous sacrifice, we at least ought to show love to others. Let's love them into the kingdom.

Prayer:

Dear God, my Father, I love You so much. Thank You that You love me, too. I cannot imagine having to give up a child as a sacrifice for all mankind, but You did. I cannot fathom that kind of love. Help me to love You more. Give me revelation of Your love and help me to do Your will. I pray in Jesus' name. Amen.

Love

Read Ephesians 4:1-7.

"Dear friends, let us love one another, for love comes from God. Everyone who loves has been born of God and knows God. Whoever does not love does not know God, because God is love" (*New International Version*, 1 John 4.7-8).

Every time I go out the front door, I am reminded of a selfless act of love that my daughter did for me. It brings a smile to my lips and joy to my heart! I do not have a green thumb! The only plants that I do not kill are plastic! My daughter even researched a plant that is hard to kill and bought it for me. When I tried to transplant it, it died.

One day she called me to say that someone gave her some plants, and she did not need them all. She asked if she could come over to plant them for me. She showed up with about ten plants, got the shovel out of the garage, and her and my granddaughter planted them all. I did not have to do anything but water them.

Like a kid, I kept looking at these small dead-looking plants wondering when they would start growing. One day she called to say that she had some flowers to plant. She came over to plant lilies. While she was working, it started raining, but she kept planting them even in the rain!

I kept my eyes on the flowers wondering when they would grow. Recently, she came over bringing more flowers, soil, black plastic, and mulch! She spent the evening finishing the landscaping for me. I still did nothing but water the flowers!

Guess what? All the flowers have started growing and now they are finally blooming. When I walk outside, I am reminded of her love for me by the sweet thing she did. I texted her, even sending her pictures, when they started growing because I was so excited! I texted her to thank her again and to say they are blooming! It brings joy to my heart because of her act of love.

I've heard it said that love is a verb, and that is the perfect example of it! Like my daughter, let us not just tell others that we love them, let us show them!

Prayer:

Dear Heavenly Father, Jesus is our example of showing love. He associated with the lowly, weak, poor, hurting, sick, and sinners. He poured out His love to them by loving them and healing them. May I be more like Him, ever mindful of those who need to know God's love. Make me sensitive to the Holy Spirit so that I can be more compassionate. May I use my talents and hobbies to encourage others. Help me to not be selfish. I pray in Jesus' name. Amen.

Let Your Light Shine

Read Matthew 5:16.

"'As the Father has sent me, I am sending you.' And with that he breathed on them and said, 'Receive the Holy Spirit'" (*New International Version*, John 20.21-22).

One summer a coworker's husband was diagnosed with a serious heart problem, so I sent her a card and wrote an encouraging letter to her. I told her how God had brought me through a difficult situation in my family. I told her how the Word had encouraged me during that time. Later, she shared with me that the letter so ministered to her that she often reread it. Her husband ended up living and having a healthy life. We ended up becoming friends and even went to a conference together. We meet and prayed together often at lunch.

Our mission as Christians is to tell others about Jesus. Let our lights shine, so others will see our good works and glorify the Father. We should tell others about the love of God and His forgiveness! I am an introvert and somewhat shy, so it is scary for me to witness to others. I do not preach on a street corner. I do not pass out tracts, but I will serve others or speak and pray with them.

In this instance, all I did was send a card. God used me to encourage someone, and her life was changed because she sought God during a difficult time. What simple acts of compassion can you do to reach out to others? Today I am sending more cards and calling to check on people. Living a life for Christ is simple. Just be led by the Spirit of God and then obey.

Prayer:

Dear Heavenly Father, Thank You for Your great love for us. Thank You for the forgiveness of sin. Thank You for Jesus and the sacrifice that He paid on the cross for my sin. Holy Spirit, guide me and show me how to live a life of godliness, compassion, and forgiveness. May I see others how You see them. May I respond and help others how You would. May I express compassion and forgiveness to others. I pray in Jesus name. Amen.

My Identity in Christ

Read Matthew 9:35-38.

"Be kind to one another, tenderhearted, forgiving one another, as God in Christ forgave you" (*New International Version*, Ephesians 4.32).

Back in November of 2003, my dad suffered one major health problem after another. First, he had a quadruple heart bypass. Ten days later, he suffered a stroke. Shortly after the stroke, while in the hospital with pancreatitis, he got Guillain-Barre Syndrome. This was all in a month's time. He wasn't able to walk because of the Guillain-Barre. One minute, he could walk, but the next minute he could not.

He spent the next two months being treated in a Springfield Hospital. It was a long road. He ended up spending two months in the hospital even at Christmas. This was after he had already been in the hospital for several weeks in November.

While he was in Springfield, which was a three-hour drive from our home, my mom never left his side except to sleep or eat. My sister, brother, and I never left her alone either. One of us was always there. My dad finally came home but had to have months of therapy to learn to walk again. He miraculously returned to work in April.

It's times like these when you learn what Christmas is really about. It is not about the presents. It is about love and commitment. Love causes you to sit by your loved one for days and months at the hospital. Love causes you to drive back and forth three hours one-way to stay with family. Love is family and friends driving hours to just to visit. Love is your church family praying for you. Love is a sister driving from Chicago or a friend driving all the way from Arizona. Love is people sending cards, money, and calling on the phone. Love is a wife never giving up on you, sitting by your side day after day, hour after hour. Love is selflessly doing what you have to do without complaining.

Jesus was our example. He loved. He cared. He wept. He healed. He was compassionate. He was a friend. Now, He is our Savior and Lord. Let's be like Jesus-spread some love.

Prayer:

Dear Heavenly Father, thank You for the love You gave through Jesus, Your Son. May I be compassionate like Jesus. Show me who needs Your love today. Thank You for family and friend that love me. I pray in Jesus' name. Amen.

Peacekeeper

Read Luke 2:14; Romans 5:1, 12:18, 14:19.

"Finally, brethren, rejoice, be made complete, be comforted, be like-minded, live in peace; and the God of love and peace will be with you" (*New International Version*, 2 Corinthians 13.11).

I hate strife and conflict. I'm always the first to say I am sorry and to try to smooth things over. I also always take up for the underdog. God made me this way. There are times when I try to stay mad at my husband and not talk to him, but after five minutes, I have forgotten all about it. I cannot stay mad. I am a peacemaker. God is the ultimate peacemaker. We were once separated from God, but he brought us peace through his Son, Jesus.

Being a peacemaker is more than trying to get people to get along. As Christians, we can bring peace into any situation by sharing Jesus. God is the God of peace. It makes sense that He would want us to walk in it and share it. In a hospital room, people need to know Jesus is our healer. In a stressful situation, people need to know Jesus is our peace. When someone wants to quit smoking, introduce him to Jesus, our Deliverer. In a lonely situation, people need to know Jesus is our friend. When someone is grieving, they need to know Jesus is our comforter. Do not just try to fix relationships between people but tell them the greatest relationship in the world is with Jesus, our Savior.

Prayer:

God of peace, thank You for Your peace that You have given to us. May I boldly share that peace with others. In Jesus' name, I pray. Amen.

Love, not Judge

Read John 8; Luke 6:37.

"And Jesus said, 'I do not condemn you either. Go on your way and from now on sin no more'" (*New International Version*, John 8.11).

I always saw things as black and white. I always thought I had to perform and do right to make God love me. Seeing sin all around me made me run away from it. Now that I am learning more about God, I have to be less sin conscience and more love conscious. God has convicted me of walking around in judgment rather than love. I was basing my thoughts on the Old Testament when they had to live by the law. That is not the case anymore.

The New Testament says that God is love and that we are to love. We love Him because He first loved us. He loved us while we were yet sinners. Jesus loved others. When others tried to condemn the woman who had an affair, He said, "He without sin cast the first stone." Of course, no one did. Then Jesus said to the woman in John 8:12, "I do not condemn you either. Go on your way and from now on sin no more" (*New International Version*).

The two greatest commandments are to love God with all your heart, soul, mind, and strength, and love your neighbor as yourself. I want to walk in love, not judgment. I want to see the need and help. I want to be helpful, not hurtful. I want to see with new eyes-see how Jesus would see, love how Jesus would love, reach out to help others. How can we show love to others?

Prayer:

Lord, help me to see through eyes of love, not condemnation or judgment. Help me not be critical of others. Let me love others for You. Give me the wisdom and discernment to be helpful and kind to others. When I start being critical, please remind me of God's love and grace. In Jesus' name. Amen.

Love Others

Read 1 Corinthians 13:4-8.

"By this everyone will know that you are my disciples, if you love one another" (*New International Version*, John 13.35).

Our pastor keeps telling us that we need to get the church outside the four walls of the church building. You've heard it said, "Put feet to your prayers." That is exactly what he means. He encourages us to get off the pew and do something for God.

One day I heard someone else say that so many people run here or there to this church or that, to this service or that, to this Bible study or that conference, but they don't use what they have learned. It really convicted me. I've stored up all this learning from studying the Word and getting good teaching, but I'm not using it as I should.

Another thing we should do is to love others. Loving others is showing God's love. I try to do what I think is pleasing to God, but I'm not sure I love others as I should. It's easy to love my family, but to love my neighbor as myself? That's a lot harder.

What do I do now that I want to change? Each day I ask God to let me love others, even more, to know how to show them love. What can I do to show love? Being filled with the Holy Spirit is a daily thing, too. I need the Spirit to guide me, teach me, and empower me to live for Him and for His love to be shone through me. He gives me supernatural love. I can't work it up.

I want to be used of God. I know that when I am pouring out into others' lives that it fills me up. Helping others brings contentment. Being used of God is enjoyable. Doing God's will is satisfying and pleasing to God.

Prayer:

Dear Loving Father, thank You for Your great love that You poured out to mankind through Your precious Son Jesus. Thank You for Your love for me. Give me revelation of Your love for me and for others. Please fill me up with Your Holy Spirit so that I can walk in supernatural love for others.

May the love of God shine through me. Let me not judge or criticize but love. Help me not turn away from those less fortunate than I, but help me have a kind word, a helpful hand, and loving ways towards them always. Let me do Your will. In Jesus' name. Amen.

Love

Read and pray for yourself 1 Corinthians 13: 4-8.

"Love is patient, love is kind. It does not envy, it does not boast, it is not proud. It does not dishonor others, it is not self-seeking, it is not easily angered, it keeps no record of wrongs. Love does not delight in evil but rejoices with the truth. It always protects, always trusts, always hopes, always perseveres. Love never fails" *(New International Version).*

My wedding was normal for the late 70's. We had a church wedding, a punch and cake reception in the basement of the church, the guests threw rice, and we went through town honking horns afterward. I wore a beautiful white gown that I had bought at the local bridal shop. My childhood best friend, my sister, and my sister-in-law were my bridesmaids; they wore matching long, soft yellow dresses and floppy hats. My husband wore light blue tails and his groomsmen wore blue tuxedos. It was colorful; that's for sure! My six year old brother was our ring bearer, and our neighbor was our flower girl. One of my good friends and my sister sang our songs! The preacher read 1 Corinthians 13, the love chapter. We had Christian vows, exchanged rings, and a kiss. It was lovely.

These scriptures are often read at weddings. It's often taught in Marriage Retreats. It's often prayed by spouses for their own spouse, but, maybe we should be praying it for the body of Christ. Maybe we should be praying it for ourselves. I know that I really need these characteristics. I have thought all these years that I was a nice person, but does it come from a heart of love? I have found that I have been nice when it's convenient for me, and I want to change. I really want to be more than nice. I want to be motivated by a real love for others. A love like Jesus' love!

Thank God for that revelation and His power at work within

me to change. My prayer is for God to change me. I will also pray 1 Corinthians 13 for myself so that I really will love others with an agape love. Join me in praying for love to be your motivator. Pray 1 Corinthians aloud. Use different versions when you pray, too. Let's see how God changes us!

Prayer:

God, forgive me for my selfishness. Help me to walk in real love towards others. Help me to see beyond sin and to see the sinner. Help me to see the lost souls that You want to reach. Give me an unselfish love for them. I pray in Jesus' name. Amen.

The Cross Brings Life

Read Matthew 27-28.

"After the Sabbath, as the first light of the new week dawned, Mary Magdalene and the other Mary came to keep vigil at the tomb. Suddenly the earth reeled and rocked under their feet as God's angel came down from heaven, came right up to where they were standing. He rolled back the stone and then sat on it. Shafts of lightning blazed from him. His garments shimmered snow-white. The guards at the tomb were scared to death. They were so frightened, they couldn't move.

The angel spoke to the women: 'There is nothing to fear here. I know you're looking for Jesus, the One they nailed to the cross. He is not here. He was raised, just as he said. Come and look at the place where he was placed'" (*The Message,* Matthew 28.1-4).

Imagine following a godly man that heals the sick, raises the dead, and ministers to all who seek Him. He claims to be the Son of God! Wherever He goes, people are radically changed, but He is put to death. How in the world can that happen? How can His ministry be stopped so suddenly after only three years? If only He had ten years, twenty, or fifty years on earth, imagine the impact! How could this happen? Why?

It happened for you and for me! He could have left for Heaven at any time. He didn't have to come to earth and be a man. He chose to come to earth to die on a cross for you and me. He chose to fulfill God's plan to save mankind. He chose to die for us! He chose to die on a cross taking our sin, guilt, and shame. Now, we don't have to pay the price or live by the Old Testament laws. Thank God for that!

We can be like Jesus on the earth. We can reach out to others like He did. We can be His vessels to love others, and set others free like He did. The Holy Spirit is sent to all those who are saved. We have the power of God to affect the world generation after generation.

Tell others the good news of Jesus. He didn't just die on a cross; He became a sacrifice for us. Then, He rose from the dead! He is alive! His death brought us life! We should be telling others the Good News.

Prayer:

Dear Heavenly Father, thank You for Your great love for us. Thank You for the plan You had to save us. Thank you for my salvation through Jesus Christ. May I have the opportunity to tell others of Your great love for us. Help me to imitate Christ by loving others, showing compassion, sharing the good news, and praying for them. May I be available to go where You urge, say what You want, and bring life into situations and people who need it. I pray this in Jesus' name. Amen.

Tell it on the Mountain

Luke 8:26-39.

"'Return home and tell how much. God has done for you.' So the man went away and told all over town how much Jesus had done for him" (*New International Version*, Luke 8.39).

When our baseball or softball teams win a state or regional ball tournament, they return home and parade through town honking horns. The fire truck leads the way, and others join the caravan, too. They may ride in the school bus, or they will ride in the back of a pickup truck. Since we are such a small town, they want everyone to celebrate with them. It is always exciting!

Jesus delivered the man in this passage from an evil spirit. He was set free to live again. Naturally, he wanted to go with Jesus, but Jesus instructed him to go home and tell others what God had done. He wouldn't have to tell much. His behavior and appearance would have been enough to show people the wonderful thing God had done.

When you meet God, He totally changes you so you want to go tell others. In Mark 15:16, Jesus commanded us to go. He said to them, "Go into all the world and preach the gospel to all creation" (*New International Version*).

What has God done in your life? Who do you need to tell? Now go and tell others what God has done for you.

Prayer:
Heavenly Father, You have done so much for me. I am so thankful for not only Your love but the gift of eternal life. You

have given me peace and have provided my every need. In times of trouble, You help me through and give me peace. Thank You, Lord. In Jesus' name. Amen.

Chapter 8: Overcoming Fear

Transformation

Read Acts 1:8; Ezekiel 36:26; Romans 12:2; Ephesians 4:22-24; 2 Corinthians 5:17; Colossians 1:21-22.

For God hath not given us the spirit of fear; but of power, and of love, and of a sound mind (*King James Version,* 2 Timothy 1.7).

I grew up in a loving family. Even today I hug my parents, brother, and sister every time I see them. I have always felt loved and accepted by my family, but something had a hold of me that prevented me from living life fully: fear. I was really shy because I was afraid of what people thought of me. I was afraid of rejection. What if I said something stupid, then everyone would laugh at me.

Don't call on me in class. Don't expect me to speak out on a subject. Don't make me get in front of a group or class to speak. Fear, intimidation, and rejection are not from God, but they once had a hold on me.

I wasn't totally bashful and introverted; around my family and close friends, it was easier to be myself. I acted silly around friends and family, but I was not free around others until I asked God to fill me with His Spirit. Eventually realizing how much He loves me and accepts me transformed my life.

I won't say that I am an extrovert now, but I can do anything that God gives me the strength and power to do. I am not bound by chains of fear and rejection because I know that God loves me and accepts me even when I mess up. Fear still tries to affect me at times, but I tell it to leave because as 2 Timothy 1:7 says, "God has not given me a spirit of fear but power, love, and a sound mind" (freedom from fear, intimidation, and rejection) (*King James Version*).

Who would have ever thought that a shy, little girl with low self-esteem would teach public school for over 25 years, be involved in numerous committees, teach Sunday School to adults, speak at church, and now for over 17 years be the Prayer Director at my church?! The person the enemy tried to keep from speaking is now boldly sharing God's Word! God set me free from rejection and fear. That's what I call transformation!

Prayer:

Thank you, God, for freedom. You set me free from those things that hinder me from doing Your will. Fill me with Your Spirit, so I can boldly proclaim Your Word. I rebuke a spirit of fear and know that I have power from on high to do what You call me to do. Thank you for transformation. In Jesus' name. Amen.

Focus on Him

Read Matthew 14:22-33.

"For God did not give us a spirit of timidity *or* cowardice *or* fear, but [He has given us a spirit] of power and of love and of sound judgment *and* personal discipline [abilities that result in a calm, well-balanced mind and self-control]" (*Amplified Bible,* 2 Timothy 1.7).

Walking up to the top of the stairs was unnerving, but I kept focusing on the stairs and trying not to look down as we ascended higher, higher, higher! My grandson had begged me to go down the tall water slide. The nearer I got to the top, the more my heart pounded. I really thought my heart was going to explode. My daughter grabbed my hand to calm me down. One step at a time slowly, carefully, focusing my eyes upward! Finally, I was next in line. I climbed in the back of the three-man tube, put my legs around my daughter then held on for dear life! I almost couldn't breathe I was so terrified.

We took off slowly. Rounding the first bend quickly, it seemed like the tube wasn't going to stop but keep on going over the side. Twisting and turning caused us to go up the other side. My mind screamed; I cannot take one more turn, but suddenly we entered the enclosed part of the slide. It was pitch dark, but at least we were enclosed, so I felt safer. I enjoyed the rest of the ride. Splash! We had landed at the bottom! The adrenaline rush was over! Relief rushed through me. Three generations had made it safely to the bottom!

I know it doesn't sound like much of an accomplishment, but if you knew how scared I am of heights you would understand. Fear can be so unreasonable, like going down a silly water slide. You can't talk someone out of being afraid. Trying to talk them out of it won't work. That's why my daughter held my hand, and my grandson was patient with me.

To get me up to the top to ride the slide, I had to be coaxed, encouraged, and made to feel safe. Guess what? I rode the water slide three more times, and the last time I kept my eyes open the whole time!

God is calling each of us to a greater calling. He is calling us higher, higher, higher! We must focus on Him and not the situation around us. We cannot let fear hold us back. You cannot let your fears hold you back! You can do anything with God! Get out of the boat! Push forward. Walk on the water! Stay focused. Open your eyes and look up to Jesus!!

Prayer:

Lord God, forgive me for letting fear hold me back. I want to go forward and do Your will. Help me do what You call me to do. Help me to confidently get out of the boat or the rut that I am in and go forward fixing my eyes on You. I pray in Jesus' name. Amen.

The Mountain Before You

Read 1 Samuel 17; Isaiah 41:10; Joshua 1:9; Deuteronomy 31:8.

"The LORD is my light and my salvation—whom shall I fear? The LORD is the stronghold of my life— of whom shall I be afraid?" (*New International Version*, Psalms 27.1).

When I was about ten years old, I ran home crying because a neighbor girl was being mean to me. We had been playing at the school playground across the street from my house, and the girl started being mean. I left my bicycle and ran home crying. I was scared of her. My bike was still at the school, and there was no way that I was going back to get it. My mom sent my six year old sister after it.

My sister wasn't afraid of anything-dead mice in the mousetrap, frogs, fish, worms, or big bullies. Stomping across the huge schoolyard to the playground, there went my sister. She was not one bit afraid of the bully even though she was four and half years younger and a lot smaller. She was determined to defend her sister and get my bicycle. In less than five minutes, my sister returned with my bicycle.

Remembering my little sister confidently marching across the yard to get my bike, reminds me of David and Goliath. David was just a young teen or preteen; Goliath was a nine foot tall giant, but David didn't back down. The giant looked like a mountain in front of the young boy. Wanting to fight him would seem foolish, but David wasn't afraid. He had God on his side. He confidently marched up to Goliath and said, "You come against me with sword and spear and javelin, but I come against you in the name of the LORD Almighty" (*New International Version*, 1 Samuel 17.45). We all know what happened next. A miracle! In spite of his size and strength, David defeated the giant!

112

You may have something that looks like a giant in your life. A mountain of a problem may be staring you in the face causing you to fear. Don't be fearful; instead, be confident that God is going before you to defeat it. He will bring you to the other side. What looks impossible to you is not impossible for God! Just like David, take your stand with God on your side.

Prayer:

Dear Heavenly Father, Thank You for Your faithfulness even when I lack faith. Build up my confidence in You so that I am not afraid. May I walk in faith, not fear. May I trust You, not myself. May I focus my eyes on You, not the situation. I pray in Jesus' name. Amen.

Be Not Afraid

Read Matthew 14: 22-33.

"I can do all this through him who gives me strength" (*New International Version*, Philippians 4.13).

After my Uncle died, the family asked me to officiate his funeral service. They didn't have a preacher. I was going to officiate the whole service, even at the cemetery. I prepared and prayed. Then, I felt ready to give the funeral service. I had a few stories, scriptures, and had rehearsed what to say. I had prayed many times about it.

The night before the funeral, I got terrified. There was no better word to describe it than terrified. Fear came in and bombarded me. It caused me to start shaking and crying. After praying, I declared scripture like 2 Timothy 1:7, "For God has not given me a spirit of fear, but of power and of love and of a sound mind," and Philippians 4:13, "I can do all things through Christ who strengthens me" (*New International Version*). After an hour, I finally felt better. I had to trust that I had heard God and that he would be with me.

The next day, I was a little nervous, but with God's help, I was able to give the eulogy and complete the entire service. It was very short, but several people told me afterward that it was good. A couple of others said they thought they were at church. God showed up. He was faithful. The most important thing is that death brought others to think about their eternal life. Plus, I stepped out of the boat, and God showed up!

Peter stepped out of the boat, too. He boldly took a step, then another, and another. Looking at Jesus, he was able to do the impossible until he noticed the wind and the waves. It was scary. When he noticed the situation around him, it caused fear to come. He had to call out to Jesus to save him. Often when God calls us to do something, fear comes in. It brings the what ifs and the negative imaginations of what could happen, like rejection or failure. If we allow our minds and imaginations to run wild, it is certain to bring fear and intimidation. Casting down those thoughts will bring faith. Faith gets us out of the boat to do God's will. Step out of the boat and watch what God does!

Prayer:

Almighty God, help me to hear You clearly and obey. May I not be sidetracked or hindered by fear. I want to get out of the boat and walk on water; I can only do that with Your help. Thank you for the Holy Spirit in me that gives me strength and power to do Your will. I am thankful for Your constant strength, grace, and Word. In Jesus' name. Amen.

Chapter 9: Being Thankful

Rejoice

Read Acts 16:25-34.

"Rejoice in the Lord always; again I will say, rejoice!" (*New International Version,* Philippians 4.4).

"The steadfast of mind You will keep in perfect peace because he trusts in You. Trust in the Lord forever, for in God the Lord, we have an everlasting Rock" (*New International Version,* Isaiah 26.3-4).

Rejoice in the Lord always!

Even when I am going through hard times-rejoice!

Even when my finances are low-rejoice!

Even when I am had a bad report-rejoice!

Even when my marriage is crumbling-rejoice!

Even when I need healing-rejoice!

Even when I need a job-rejoice!

Even when I am stressed-rejoice!

Even when life isn't going my way-rejoice!

Even when...

Rejoicing in the Lord is necessary to make it through difficult times. God's love is constant, and He is faithful. God is at work in your situation. Rejoicing in the hard times not only changes your attitude but changes the atmosphere around you, just like Paul and Silas. That's what walking in faith is all about.

116

It's not about agreeing with your negative circumstances, but it's seeing beyond them to believe that God is at work.

Did Paul and Silas worry about being in jail? Did they stress out? Did they dwell on the negative? Did they complain or have a pity party? Were they afraid? No, they rejoiced in their God because they believed in Him and had a relationship with Him.

What situation are you in right now? Are you praising God in the midst of it? Remember Paul and Silas were in jail and praising God when the chains came off, and they were set free! Not only that, but the guard and his whole household were saved. Are you praising and thanking God for His peace in the midst of the storm? Are you reading your Bible and having quiet time so you can hear from God in the midst of the rocking boat as the waves pound against you. Now sit in God's peaceful presence. He has all you need.

"It is not the dead who praise the LORD, those who go down to the place of silence; it is we who extol the LORD, both now and forevermore. Praise the LORD" (*New International Version,* Psalm 115.17-18).

Prayer:

Lord God, life is often painful and difficult. I go through difficult times and find myself worried, afraid, or complaining when I should be praising You and thanking You. I need a new perspective to see You at work and believe that You are here with me. Help me to walk by faith. I pray in Jesus' name. Amen.

Be Thankful

Read Philippians 4:6.

"Enter his gates with thanksgiving and his courts with praise" (*New International Version,* Psalm 100.4).

"I will praise the name of God with song, And shall magnify Him with thanksgiving" (*New International Version,* Psalm 69.30).

"Therefore as you have received Christ Jesus the Lord, so walk in Him, having been firmly rooted and now being built up in Him and established in your faith, just as you were instructed, and overflowing with gratitude" (*New International Version,* Colossians 2.6-7).

"I will bless the LORD at all times; His praise shall continually be in my mouth" (*New International Version,* Psalm 34.1).

"Enter His gates with thanksgiving, And His courts with praise. Give thanks to Him; bless His name" (*New International Version,* Psalm 100.4).

Thessalonians 5.18).

I try to read my Bible and pray every morning. Sometimes, my prayers sound more like a Christmas list asking God for many things for myself, my loved ones, and others rather than adoration, worship, and thankfulness. I tend to start off praising God and loving on Him; then, I start down the list. It is usually because I am in a hurry.

For a season, God told me not to ask for anything on Tuesdays. Do you know how hard that is? There are so many needs and so many people sick that it is hard not to ask for anything, but I obeyed. Instead of asking, I started thanking God. While thinking about all the blessings that I have, I could thank Him for hours. Tuesdays turned into a sweet time in God's presence; not only was I thanking Him for what I already had but also for what I was believing He would do in my life and others.

Let's be a little more grateful for our blessings and what God is doing in our lives and the lives of others. Even Jesus thanked the Father. He is our example. We should be very thankful.

Prayer:

Dear Father God, I am so thankful for all the blessings in my life. You have saved my soul, filled me with Your spirit, and set me free. Thank You for the sacrifice of Your son, Jesus. Thank You for Your love for me. I love and adore You. In Jesus' name. Amen.

Glorious Creator

Read Acts 4:18-22.

"Worthy are You, our Lord and our God, to receive glory and honor and power; for You created all things, and because of Your will they existed, and were created" (*New International Version*, Revelation 4.11).

All the people were praising God because the lame man was healed. It was a miracle that all could see. How can you stop people from praising God when they have seen the great things He has done?

A friend and I were running down her country road to the church and back. We were enjoying the cool, quiet morning. There was not much traffic. The grass and trees were glistening green with dew. The birds were chirping their morning songs. Several baby buffalo were grazing in a small herd. We saw a log across the creek, and we wondered how many animals used it to cross over the creek. It was just a glorious day to remind us of our creator!

All around me the beautiful morning pointed to God's majesty and power. I was so thankful for nature and my beautiful Creator!

Prayer:
Thank you, Lord God, Creator of all things! Thank You for this beautiful day, the coolness of the breeze and the beauty of nature. Thank You for Your handiwork that I see all around in the beauty of nature like the sun and moon, the forest and river, the waterfall, the rabbits, the birds soaring through the air, and baby rabbits. I am so grateful to get to experience You in creation. I pray in Jesus' name. Amen.

Praise God

Read Psalm 98, 100.

"Let everything that has breath praise the Lord. Praise the Lord!" (*New International Version*, Psalm 150.6).

I love music! Everyone has a type of music they like best. I grew up in the 70s, so I know all of that music. Now that I am older and hear some of those lyrics, I can't believe that I still know the words.

Now I listen to music that is uplifting and meaningful to me. I listen to Christian music or praise and worship music. When I say that, people often think of hymns, but Christian music has different genres just like other music. I love the hymns that I sang as a child. Now I like the more contemporary music that has a beat that can get my toe tapping and me singing along. I love worship music, too. It is more soothing; it causes me to reflect on Jesus, His love for me, and my love for Him. It often moves me to thank God or pray.

The book of Psalms is full of verses of praise and worship to God. David loved to sing, play the lyre, and dance before God. David was considered a man after God's heart. David wasn't afraid to express his love for God in praise and worship.

I love my church because we can clap and dance if we want. The music is what drew me to my church. I pray quite a lot at home, but I often forget to thank God and praise Him. I want to be more like David. I want to praise God. I want to be a woman after His heart. We should take time to praise God today.

Prayer:

Great and Mighty God, You are awesome. Help me remember to praise You in all things. You have given me wonderful blessings. I am so thankful for all You've given me. I praise You for Your love, Your faithfulness, the sacrifice of Your son, Jesus, and Your constant presence. I love You so much. In Jesus' name. Amen.

Memories

Read Genesis 12:1-9.

"I will remember the deeds of the LORD; yes, I will remember your miracles of long ago. I will consider all your works and meditate on all your mighty deeds" (*New International Version*, Psalm 77.11-12).

Most of my memories are of everyday things. Some are good and a few are bad memories. Falling on my bike and getting rocks in my knees, having a bad earache so I had to go to the doctor, getting hit in the head with a hairspray can while playing war with the neighborhood boys resulting in stitches (I still have the scar), and my uncle passing away are all some of my earlier bad memories.

My second grade birthday party, playing at school, playing with friends, playing Barbie dolls, dancing, and swimming are some of my good memories. Then those satisfying memories of stories being read to me at bedtime, eating at Grandma's house with all my aunts, uncles, and cousins, and going on vacation with my family. Memories are important to me; that's why I take pictures and write them down.

Abraham built altars when he encountered God. The altars were like pictures for him. They helped him remember the encounters he experienced at those special places. Those places held significant memories that impacted his life. They were milestones in his life. He needed and wanted to remember them.

It's beneficial to remember the good and learn from the past. Be thankful for your memories. Think of what God has done in your life. Remember the events that shaped your life. Now I want to continue making good memories for my children and grandchildren.

Prayer:

God, please help me to be a positive influence in my children's lives. I pray that they have pleasant memories. I am thankful for the memories of my life. Help me to remember the significant memories. Help me continue to build good memories in my life and with my family. I pray in Jesus' name. Amen.

Works Cited

"Courage." *iBooks,* Apple Inc., 2016.

Hillsong United. "Oceans (Where Feet May Fail)." *Zion,* Sparrow, 2013.

McKeown, Greg. *Essentialism: The Disciplined Pursuit of Less.* McKeown, Inc, *2017.*

Mollenhauer, Heidi. "God Help the Outcasts," *The Hunchback of Notre Dame,* Written by Alan Menken and Stephen Schwartz, Walt Disney Records, 1996.

Mullen, Nicole C. "My Redeemer Lives," *Redeemer: The Best Of Nicole C. Mullen,* Word Entertainment, 2006.

"Redeem." *Merriam-Webster,* Encyclopedia Britannica, 2016.

"Redeemer." *Merriam-Webster,* Encyclopedia Britannica, 2016.

The Holy Bible. Amplified Bible, The Lockman Foundation, 2015.

The Holy Bible. Living Bible, Tyndale House Foundation, 1971.

The Holy Bible. King James Version, Biblica, Inc, 2016.

The Holy Bible. New International Version, Biblica, Inc, 2011.

The Holy Bible. NIV Once-A-Day Bible for Women, Zondervan, 2012.

The Holy Bible, The Message, edited by Eugene H. Peterson, NavPress Publishing Group, 2002.

Williams, Pamela Rose. "15 Christian Quotes about Fasting." *What Christians Want to Know: Topics to Equip, Encourage & Energize.* 2014.

Get your *L.I.F.E. Apps Journal* that goes along with this devotion on Amazon.

Be looking for the next books written by this author. More *L.I.F.E. Apps devotions* will be published next year. The next books in the series will consist of shorter applications or devotions with scripture to encourage you to Live in Faith Everyday along with a journal.

Be looking for the author's children's books to be published soon- *Cooper's Mini Adventure* a cute story about a turtle that learns never to give up and a cute rhyming book *Nonna Lost her Keys*.

www.tammytrusty.com

Made in the USA
Lexington, KY
21 November 2019

57333883R00074